The Faith of Joh

The Faith of
John Dryden

❧ Change and Continuity ❧

G. DOUGLAS ATKINS

THE UNIVERSITY PRESS OF KENTUCKY

Library of Congress Cataloging in Publication Data

Atkins, George Douglas, 1943–
    The faith of John Dryden.

    Includes bibliographical references and index.
    1. Dryden, John, 1631–1700—Religion and ethics.
I. Title.
PR3427.R4A8   821'.4   80-12890
ISBN 0-8131-1401-2

Scholarly publisher for the Commonwealth,
serving Berea College, Centre College of Kentucky,
Eastern Kentucky University, The Filson Club,
Georgetown College, Kentucky Historical Society,
Kentucky State University, Morehead State University,
Murray State University, Northern Kentucky University,
Transylvania University, University of Kentucky,
University of Louisville, and Western Kentucky University.

Editorial and Sales Offices: Lexington, Kentucky 40506

For my mother, my father,
and my wife

Contents

Preface

This is a study of Dryden's religious positions from beginning to end, of the changing patterns of his thought, and of the development in understanding that led him eventually to the Church of Rome. Because we must derive Dryden's religious positions from the expression of ideas primarily in poems and plays, study of these positions involves, if not becomes, study of his art. Because the art embodying these positions is inseparable from the mind that created it, I have woven together, however clumsily, textual criticism, biography, and historical scholarship. Though I have a good deal to say about intellectual contexts, particularly in discussing the perennial issue of the conversion, my principal concern is with foreground, not background.

The attempt to treat the entire range of Dryden's work, not simply the two major religious poems, and to attend to the artistic expression of the ideas involved has brought to the fore issues previously slighted. One of the most important of these is the continuing tension between Dryden and the priesthood and the church and his concomitant efforts on behalf of his fellow laity. As it marks an important point in the evolution of his religious thinking, *Religio Laici* directs us both backward and forward in time to that continuing desire to formulate a layman's faith. This continuity in concern provides a way of tracing and evaluating changes in religious position, including the much-discussed conversion to Roman Catholicism. Thus I begin with *Religio Laici* and return to the poem in Chapter Four.

My interests in this study being what I have described, I have not sought to offer a comprehensive account of Dryden's religious thought. Mine, I hope, will be groundwork for future such studies, which will need to consider issues I have scanted. I should also say that it will no doubt appear to some readers that I have at points allowed the distance to collapse between Dryden and myself. I have done so deliberately, believing that we should go all the way with authors we study, allowing them to have their way with us. I am talking, of course, about sympathetic involvement, not final agreement. I think Dryden can be understood only from an "inside" perspective.

Portions of this study have previously appeared in journals and are reprinted here with the kind permission of the respective editors: *Texas Studies in Literature and Language*, published by the University of Texas Press ("The Function and Significance of the Priest in Dryden's *Troilus and Cressida*," 13 [1971]: 29–37), *Studies on Voltaire and the Eighteenth Century* ("The Ancients, the Moderns, and Gnosticism," 151–55 [1976]: 149–66), *Cithara: Essays in the Judaeo-Christian Tradition* ("Dryden on the Priesthood: 'The Character of a Good Parson,'" 16 [1977]: 109–18), *Ball State University Forum*, © *Forum* ("Serapion's Function in *All for Love*," 19 [1978]: 35–37), and *Studies in Philology* ("Dryden's *Religio Laici*: A Reappraisal," 75 [1978]: 347–70).

During the years I have studied Dryden I have been very fortunate in the institutions and individuals who have generously supported my work. It is a pleasure to acknowledge my indebtedness and to express my gratitude. The University of Kansas has been unfailing in providing various kinds of assistance including grants from the General Research Fund, a sabbatical leave, and aid in the preparation of the manuscript. At a crucial stage of my work the William Andrews Clark Memorial Library awarded me a postdoctoral fellowship. Later the American Council of Learned Societies provided a grant-in-aid, which made possible additional work at the Clark and Huntington libraries. I want to make special mention of the genial helpfulness of the staff of the Clark Library. My debt to previous writers on Dryden is great but no doubt inadequately acknowledged in the notes. I wish to acknowledge the generous help with the proofreading given by Laurie P. Morrow and Geraldo Udex de Sousa. I should like to express my deep gratitude to the following individuals from whose encouragement, advice, assistance, and example I have benefited enormously: Irvin Ehrenpreis and Arthur C. Kirsch, readers of the dissertation on Dryden and the clergy, in which I made some faltering, inchoate steps toward a book; my colleagues at Kansas, especially David M. Bergeron and Joel J. Gold; and certainly not least, Aubrey Williams, mentor and friend, who prodded constantly but always mercifully and without whose sustaining faith and example I simply would not have persevered. Despite their considerable, often direct, contributions to this study I alone bear responsibility for errors of fact, interpretation, and taste. To them, to my parents, to my daughter Leslie and my son Christopher, and to my wife Jean, this is pitifully small compensation for so much given.

A Note on Texts

I have used the authoritative *Works of John Dryden*, ed. E. N. Hooker, H. T. Swedenberg, Jr., et al. (Berkeley: University of California Press, 1956–), cited throughout as *Works*, for the poems, plays, and prose works (other than critical) so far available in this edition and have given full bibliographical particulars for the respective volumes in the notes. For poems not yet available in this edition I have gone to *The Poems of John Dryden*, ed. James Kinsley, 4 vols. (Oxford: Clarendon Press, 1958), with citations identified by "K," and for plays not yet published in the California Edition to *The Works of John Dryden*, ed. Sir Walter Scott, rev. and corr. George Saintsbury, 18 vols. (Edinburgh, 1883–1892), with citations identified by act and scene, rather than by act, scene, and line, as with the California Edition. For the sake of convenience in dealing with the critical essays I have relied on the Everyman Library edition, *"Of Dramatic Poesy" and Other Critical Essays*, ed. George Watson, 2 vols. (New York: Dutton, 1962).

1

Approaching Dryden's Religious Thought

The scholarly view of John Dryden's thought has changed radically since 1934. That year Louis I. Bredvold published *The Intellectual Milieu of John Dryden*,[1] which transformed the way both specialists and general readers regarded the man and the poet and determined the direction of Dryden studies for decades. Specifically, Bredvold identified what Dryden termed his inclination to "Scepticism in Philosophy" (in the Preface to *Religio Laici*) with the centuries-old tradition of philosophical skepticism, or Pyrrhonism, fundamentally distrustful of the human reason. This temperament, he argued, was particularly vulnerable to the claims of Roman Catholicism, whose thought in the seventeenth century he found to be fideistic. On this argument it was possible to contend that Dryden's conversion to the Church of Rome, only a few months after the accession of James II, was not the product of a time-serving nature but the result of a long search for infallible authority, rather than fallible reason, in matters of religion. Signs of this development Bredvold located four years before conversion in *Religio Laici*, which he interpreted as crypto-Catholic. As a result of Bredvold's work many of the most persistent charges bruited against Dryden were silenced. For he not only laid to rest the claims that the conversion was inconsistent, insincere, and merely opportunistic, but he also demonstrated Dryden's longtime interest in serious religious questions, the capaciousness of his mind, the depth of his understanding, and the integrity and quality of his artistic productions.

For over a quarter of a century Bredvold's argument was accepted by editors, biographers, and other scholars as the authoritative statement on Dryden's religious thought.[2] The first serious challenge to Bredvold's authority came in 1961 when two scholars working independently questioned his interpretation of Dryden's position on the power of reason as well as his reading of *Religio Laici;* Thomas H. Fujimura argued that the poem is an orthodox Anglican work, while Elias J. Chiasson sought to place its author within the tradition of "Anglican Christian humanism."[3] This challenge received valuable support in 1968 with the publication of Phillip Harth's *Contexts of Dryden's Thought,* the first book on Dryden's religious thinking since 1934. Like Chiasson and Fujimura, Harth found Dryden's first major religious poem to be based, as the poet claimed in his Preface, in Anglican apologetics. Rather than with fideists, therefore, Harth aligned Dryden with "Anglican rationalists," or Latitudinarians, like Tillotson and Stillingfleet who, though they rejected the idea that reason could demonstrate or comprehend the mysteries of religion, believed that it performs a necessary function in religion. The troublesome skepticism, Harth demonstrated, was not at all a theory of knowledge, as Bredvold had supposed, but only a mode of inquiry like the antidogmatism practiced by the scientists of the Royal Society.[4]

Subsequent work on Dryden's religious positions has continued the attack on Bredvold, claiming that Dryden was never an antirationalist. In *Dryden and the Abyss of Light,* Sanford Budick argues the poet's continuing debt to the Cambridge Platonists and their "complex doctrine of man's innate capacity for saving truths."[5] In articles even more recently published, R. W. McHenry, Jr., aligns Dryden with the traditional concept "right reason," and William Empson, in more extreme fashion, links Dryden with the Deists.[6]

Regrettably, the necessary task of modifying Bredvold has led to more than one extreme position and to the blurring of im-

portant distinctions. I do not believe that Dryden can unprob-
lematically be aligned with the Church of England, nor with
rationalism. In the course of this study I hope to demonstrate
these points. I should like to begin this demonstration by discussing the work central to all major studies of Dryden's religious positions, *Religio Laici*. A preliminary discussion of the
poem at this point will allow me to suggest a new approach to
the large issue of Dryden's religious thought. The poem reflects,
I think, a struggle then under way in Dryden himself and contains seemingly contradictory impulses which, when only one is
emphasized, lead easily to very different interpretations, such as
those of Bredvold and his recent opponents.

Despite, for example, Budick's insistence that the poem be
treated as poetry, a highly regarded view is that *Religio Laici* is
not only rooted in orthodox Anglican rationalism but also intended as a conventional apologia, addressed "exclusively" to
the poet's fellow Anglicans in hopes of preventing further defec-
tions from that church. Such an interpretation apparently stems
from confusing Dryden's vehicle for his meaning and neglecting
the difference between theology and the poetic meaning theology has been used to construct. At any rate, especially when the
poetry of *Religio Laici* is confined to the "dress" added to a "logical structure," the effect is to reduce the poem to the level of
hundreds of commonplace prose tracts.[7] Such an assessment is
far different from that of most readers of the poem.

The history of commentary on *Religio Laici*, in fact, reveals
the singularity in interpreting it as an apologia. Dr. Johnson, for
example, thought the poem "almost the only work of Dryden
which can be considered as a voluntary effusion," and David
Nichol Smith has similarly called *Religio Laici* a "wholly spon-
taneous" poem in which Dryden "assumes 'an honest layman's
liberty' and argues out his problems for the peace of his own
mind."[8] Like many others, Arthur W. Hoffman, in an illuminat-
ing discussion of the poetry of *Religio Laici*, has described it as
simply the expression of a layman's faith.[9] Countless other commentators from the eighteenth century forward could be cited,

but more telling, I think, is the fact that none of the several contemporary statements on *Religio Laici* discusses it as an apologia for any church. Importantly, several of these early accounts go beyond Nichol Smith and Hoffman, believing that *because* it is a layman's faith the poem has a particular meaning. For example, in a little-known pamphlet entitled *Religio Laici, Or A Lay-mans Faith, Touching the Supream Head And Infallible Guide Of The Church . . .* (1688), J. R., a "Convert of Mr. Bays's," writes:

> You have neither spar'd cost nor pains, but have been extravagantly lavish in Painting your (beloved) Priests; but I presume the Reason was your Charity to your poor Brethren the Laity, that they might beware of having any thing to do with them, and that possible [sic] might induce you to publish your own Creed in 82, giving it the Title of the *Lay-mans Faith*, in which you insinuate the unreasonableness of pinning our Faith upon the Priests Sleeves; and truly as to that you have made an absolute Convert of me, for I am much of your mind . . . yet I must needs confess I am not altogether of your Judgment, for I am willing to believe there are Priests of some Religions that are very honest and have no ill designs: But your *Religio Laici* has made me almost of your Perswasion.[10]

As an attack on Dryden's Catholic position on the church, this interpretation might be dismissed were it not for the similar views expressed by Dryden's friends in the introductory poems in the earliest editions of *Religio Laici*.[11] According to the unsigned first poem, probably by John Lord Vaughan, to whom Dryden had dedicated *The Kind Keeper* two years before:

> Too long has captiv'd Reason been enslav'd,
> By Visions scar'd, and airy Phantasms brav'd,
> Listning t' each proud Enthusiastick Fool,
> Pretending Conscience, but designing Rule;
> Whilst Law, Form, Interest, Ignorance, Design,
> Did in the holy Cheat together joyn.

Like vain Astrologers gazing on the Skyes,
We fell, and did not dare to trust our Eyes.
'Tis time at last to fix the trembling Soul,
And by thy Compass to point out the Pole.

(ll. 31–40)

Dryden's sometime-collaborator Thomas Creech makes the point even more forcefully in the second poem:

'Tis nobly done, a Layman's Creed profest,
When all our Faith of late hung on a Priest;
His doubtfull words like Oracles receiv'd,
And when we could not understand, believ'd.

(ll. 1–4)

Thanks to Dryden's efforts in *Religio Laici*, the layman has at last been freed from the shackles imposed by a tyrannical and self-seeking priesthood.

Perhaps it is because twentieth-century readers have rarely had the advantage enjoyed by Dryden's contemporaries of encountering these poems before turning to *Religio Laici* that they have missed its basic nature and direction. Fulfilling the expectations created by the title, *Religio Laici, Or A Laymans Faith*, written in the form of a Horatian epistle, belongs to the little-known seventeenth-century tradition of layman's faiths. As far as I have been able to determine, sixteen works with titles similar to Dryden's appeared between 1645 and 1695. Despite differences in purpose, scope, and style, the majority of these express a specifically lay approach to religion; most of them, in fact, show a marked antagonism toward the clergy.[12] They are far more concerned with the practice of charity than with creeds and articles of faith.

Though an aspect of the century's antiauthoritarianism, anticlericalism, and laicization of religious matters, the desire for a faith distinct from the clergy's was specifically aroused by the controversy and dissension of early and mid-century. For this situation the authors of layman's faiths blame the clergy. Religious division and public disturbance, they claim, are the inevitable result of the clergy's insistence on minor points of faith. Charles Blount, for example, who claimed to be continuing Dryden's effort a year later in his own *Religio Laici*, charges that "*our Modern* Priests (*for the most part*) *turn* Religion *into* Faction, *striving to render all others of different Perswasions (though in the least matters) odious. Which Bitterness of Spirit we find not evidently remarked among the* Heathen Priests; *so that how Ignorant and False soever they were, yet are they not recorded to have been* Incendiaries, *and* Persecutors *of one another unto* Death, *for* Religion *and* Conscience *sake.*"[13]

The laymen's suggestions for change revolve around a vigorous laicism. Progress will involve minimizing the power and authority of those who burden "the shoulders of weak Christians, with the unnecessary trash of humane invention."[14] For everywhere, declares Lord Herbert of Cherbury,

[the layman] will find the priestly order, however quarrelsome and clamorous about their faiths, however busy sowing contentions not only among themselves but among neighboring nations, conspiring together none the less about these matters: everywhere to interpose and to maintain their authority; to allow nothing they teach to be so much as doubted; to confine what is most important to abstruse and difficult passages which they interpret; to restrain the most lawful pleasures which they themselves have not appointed; to deny obstinately that heaven can be approached without their influence; to threaten anathemas and eternal punishments against those who differ; briefly, conspiring that neither entering nor leaving this world should be quite lawful without their aid.[15]

Emerging through the layman's faiths is a new, latitudinarian approach to religion. In order to end the haggling over nonessentials, which they claim is at the bottom of the contumely and dissension, the laymen will avoid "those articles which are violently disputed" and "those controversies which [the laymen] will in no age sufficiently clarify." Thus, "However the most renowned schoolmen cry out . . . the means of salvation must be sought in few doctrines, and these easily perceived."[16] Variously defined, the essentials of faith have far more to do with conduct and the practice of charity than with dogma. So, just as Blount avers "to attend a *good life,* and *repentance,*" Mackenzie declares, "My design all alongst this Discourse, butts at this one principle, that *Speculations in Religion are not so necessary, and are more dangerous then sincere practice.*"[17] Repeating the usual charges against the clergy and summarizing the position of the laymen, the author of *The Lay-Man's Religion* maintains that "the vital part of Religion" has been turned into "*Sophistry* and *Dispute,* which begets Quarrels in Professors about *Shadows* and *Circumstantials,* whilst they neglect the Substance in good Living, thereby banishing *Christian Charity.*"[18] One has but to consider the fact of Lord Herbert and Blount, both Deists, at either end of the temporal spectrum of the "tradition," to appreciate the modernist direction of the layman's faiths.

The same reasonable and balanced position appears in Dryden's poem; like the other laymen, he insists on concern with only essential points of faith, exhibits a notable spirit of charitableness alongside an opposition to religious zeal, and obviously desires quiet rather than controversy and disturbance. From the apparent similarity of many aspects of Dryden's position to orthodox Anglicanism some critics assume an identity with those doctrines, mistakenly concluding that Dryden's poetic meaning is simply and conventionally Anglican. Actually Dryden exploits Church of England doctrines for his own individualistic purposes.

Rhetorically, of course, he capitalizes on the Anglican basis of his own position, never directly separating himself from the Established Church and sometimes using the first-person plural in the Preface to link himself with her.[19] That his audience, nevertheless, is not restricted to his fellow Anglicans is established by such a passage as this: "But, by asserting the Scripture to be the Canon of our Faith, I have unavoidably created to my self two sorts of Enemies: The Papists indeed, more directly, because they have kept the Scripture from us, what they cou'd." Were he addressing Anglicans, there would be no need to assert that Scripture is the "Canon" of their faith, since that was universally understood and accepted by Anglicans. Moreover, the phrasing that follows suggests the individualism behind the sentence: his effort is new, and so it "creates" two sorts of opponents. Finally, lines 370–91 in the poem, detailing the pre-Reformation impositions on laymen, gloss this passage, make clear Dryden's referent above, and illustrate defining characteristics of the kind of work he is writing:

> In times o'ergrown with Rust and Ignorance,
> A gainfull Trade their Clergy did advance:
> When want of Learning kept the *Laymen* low,
> And none but *Priests* were *Authoriz'd* to *know:*
> When what small Knowledge was, in them did dwell;
> And he a *God* who cou'd but *Reade* or *Spell;*
> Then *Mother Church* did mightily prevail:
> She parcel'd out the Bible by *retail:*
> But still *expounded* what She *sold* or *gave;*
> To keep it in her *Power* to *Damn* and *Save:*
> *Scripture* was *scarce,* and as the Market went,
> Poor *Laymen* took *Salvation* on *Content;*
> As needy men take Money, good or bad:
> *God's* Word they had not, but the *Priests* they had.
> Yet, whate'er *false Conveyances* they made,
> The *Lawyer* still was *certain* to be paid.
> In those dark times they learn'd their knack so well,
> That by long use they grew *Infallible:*
> At last, a knowing Age began t' enquire
> If *they* the *Book,* or *That* did *them* inspire:
> And, making narrower search they found, thô late,
> That what they thought the *Priest's,* was *Their* Estate.

Because the work is a layman's faith, tension and conflict exist in both poem and Preface between the clergy and the layman-poet. This is apparent from the very beginning, where

Dryden acknowledges the boldness of his effort. But in attempting to head off the expected charge of presumptuousness Dryden denies that his subject is the special province of divines:

> In the first place, if it be objected to me that being a *Layman*, I ought not to have concern'd my self with Speculations, which belong to the Profession of *Divinity*; I cou'd Answer, that perhaps, Laymen, with equal advantages of Parts and Knowledge, are not the most incompetent Judges of Sacred things; But in the due sense of my own weakness and want of Learning, I plead not this: I pretend not to make my self a Judge of Faith, in others, but onely to make a Confession of my own; I lay no unhallow'd hand upon the Ark; but wait on it, with the Reverence that becomes me at a distance.

Clearly, the passage is both defensive and assertive and recalls Dryden's more forthright statement of the ties between poetry and religion in the Preface to *Tyrannick Love* (1670): "to leave the employment [of precepts and examples of piety] altogether to the clergy were to forget that religion was first taught in verse (which the laziness or dullness of succeeding priesthood turned afterwards into prose)."[20] Here Dryden implies that properly qualified laymen have a right to treat sacred matters. But, having insinuated this claim on behalf of certain others, Dryden distinguishes between the alleged boldness but actual freedom of qualified laymen to discuss substantive religious issues and the undoubted presumptuousness that would lead from this to a proud attempt to control divine and human laws.

Continuing his defense Dryden claims, as was conventional in layman's faiths, not only that his arguments are respectable because drawn largely from the works of Anglican divines but also that he is willing to refer his personal opinions "with all reverence to my Mother Church, accounting them no further mine, than as they are Authoriz'd, or at least, uncondemn'd by her."[21] As proof he cites his precaution in showing the manuscript to "a judicious and learned Friend, a Man indefatigably

zealous in the service of the Church and State," but he adds that
that friend prudently advised him to omit his "bold" remarks on
Saint Athanasius (ll. 212–23): "But then I could not have satisfied my self, that I had done honestly not to have written what
was my own." In retaining his "bold" treatment of Athanasius
and "other faults" against this man's advice, Dryden exhibits
both a willingness to consult the church and a refusal always to
be guided by her.[22] He is not quite so submissive as he claims.

Similar tension appears in the poem's penultimate verse paragraph. This is not Dryden's explicit support of Anglicanism as
the necessary alternative to the positions already confronted in
the poem. Indeed, the argument here is significantly different
from the doctrine expressed in Anglican apologetics, particularly on the question of church authority, with which it has
been identified. The first few verses focus on individualistic self-
assertion and the unreasonable egoism that turns the present
against the past and the part against the whole, with Dryden insisting that

> In doubtfull questions 'tis the safest way
> To learn what unsuspected Ancients say:
> For 'tis not likely *we* shou'd higher Soar
> In search of Heav'n, than *all the Church before.*
>   (ll. 435–38)

In the remaining verses he continues to defer to common understanding and to inveigh against self-assertion, now appearing as
the "private reason," but in so doing he reveals some important
differences with Anglican apologetics.

> Nor can we be deceiv'd, unless we see
> The *Scripture,* and the *Fathers disagree.*
> If after all, they stand suspected still,
> (For no man's Faith depends upon his Will;)
> 'Tis some Relief, that points not clearly known,
> Without much hazard may be let alone:
> And, after hearing what our Church can say,

If still our Reason runs another way,
That private Reason 'tis more Just to curb,
Than by Disputes the publick Peace disturb.
For points obscure are of small use to learn:
But *Common quiet* is *Mankind's concern.*

(ll. 439–50)

In support of my claim I offer passages cited as evidence of the identity of *Religio Laici* and orthodox Anglican doctrine. The first is by Henry Ferne, writing at mid-century:

Wee teach all Inferiors, whether People or Priests, when they finde cause of doubt or question against such definitions or practise [of the Established Church] to instruct their owne reason, and rather rely upon the publick Judgement then their owne in every doubtfull case. . . . If they cannot finde satisfaction so, as inwardly to acquiesce, yet to yeild externall obedience, and peaceable subjection, according as the condition of the matter questioned will bear. In a word, we require all that submission of judgment and outward compliance, that may be due to an Authority, not infallible, yet guiding others by an infallible Rule.[23]

Dryden's distance from this apologist emerges with the last two sentences, for whereas Ferne sees the church as the layman's guide the poet finds Scripture itself sufficient; as he put it earlier in the poem:

The *welcome News* is in the *Letter* found;
The *Carrier's* not Commission'd to *expound.*
It *speaks* it *Self,* and what it does contain,
In all things *needfull* to be *known,* is *plain.*

(ll. 366–69)

Dryden admits the layman should consult "what unsuspected Ancients say," for not to do so is to exhibit the willful pride he has condemned throughout the poem. But nowhere in this passage does he suggest that the layman ought "to yeild externall obedience" to the church whose opinions he privately rejects, nor does he suggest the layman should submit his judgment to the church.[24] Further, whereas the call for submission in Ferne and in Daniel Whitby, cited as expressing "Dryden's principle exactly," is predicated on the need to preserve what Whitby calls "the Churches peace," Dryden's very different plea that the layman "curb" his own "private Reason" arises from a desire for a larger "publick Peace" and a more comprehensive "*Common quiet.*"[25]

Dryden's position in *Religio Laici* is even more clearly distinct from the anonymous *Religio Clerici,* published the year before. It is possible that Dryden intended his poem as in part a reply to this tract, which itself testifies to the growth of laicism. Fundamentally different from the authors of layman's faiths, the clergyman vigorously opposes toleration and stoutly defends the Established Church. He is no more temperate regarding the position of the priesthood vis-à-vis the laity. About the increasing laicism, for example, he says, "we would not have the blind presume to teach others to see." Moreover, in direct opposition to the enlightened and inquiring spirit of the layman's faiths, he maintains that the laity are best kept "ignorant that there is any opposition in any kinde to the truth of our Doctrines: besides, what necessity is there of telling them (to their dangerous *amusement*) what is wrong, as long as we continue them in the right Belief and Practice of what we know to be true and right?" The layman's responsibility is thus clear and simple; it is to submit to clerical authority: "to follow still with generous and steadfast duty, our *Royal,* our *Noble,* our *Honourable,* and our *Reverend Learned Leaders.*"[26]

Rather than seek a limited institutional or ecclesiastical solution to current problems, *Religio Laici* works toward moral and theological ends, its opponents being in large part both the ignorance in which the laity had long been enslaved and the proud self-assertion that has followed the breaking of the shackles. Accordingly, Dryden confronts in the poem's major debates the Deist and the Catholic, rather than Deism and Catholicism, and his own character as projected in the poem embodies the norms. He alone is able to walk the dangerous tightrope between proud and willful self-sufficiency and the knowledge that comes with free access to God's Word. If, as he claims, he has made his "own Opinions clear," he has nevertheless laid "no unhallow'd hand upon the Ark." He thus exemplifies the layman's faith as Dryden now understands it: enslaved to neither private reason, the church, nor the private spirit, he is neither proud nor ignorant but obedient to Ultimate Authority as revealed in Scripture.

My argument concerning *Religio Laici* should be more persuasive when we have considered Dryden's lifelong anticlericalism. He seems to have long subscribed to the notion he finally put into words in the Preface to the *Fables:* "A satirical poet is the check of the laymen on bad priests." [27] In light of the anticlericalism, which I shall document, as well as such statements as that in the Preface to *Tyrannick Love,* quoted earlier, regarding the moral and religious duties of poetry, it may not be unreasonable to view *Religio Laici* as Dryden's attempt to accept the responsibility and perform the function that in his view a corrupt priesthood had abandoned.

Further development of these points must wait, but for now I hope enough has been said to indicate that Dryden's religious position in 1682 was not so simple as has recently been claimed. Rather than an apologist who forswears his own opinions in order to express church doctrine, Dryden appears to have been a layman who delighted in the freedom to speak his own mind and who was engaged in a running battle with the clergy, including that of his own church. If I am right, Dryden's conversion four years after his layman's faith may appear even more enigmatic than generally supposed, since Catholicism was widely believed to be "priest-ridden."

I have suggested, however, that the tension in *Religio Laici* between poet-layman and the church is subordinate to a larger aim and in fact becomes a means of insisting on absolute, rather than limited, authority. Necessarily I have here emphasized only one side of *Religio Laici,* and that, as it happens, is ul-

2

The Early
Religious Opinions

If following his conversion in late 1685 or early 1686 Dryden's religious position was clear and simple (by all accounts he remained a devout Catholic the rest of his life), his opinions before the late 1670s at least are not at all clear. For one thing, we have almost no direct biographical information on the first thirty years of Dryden's life. For another, his position from 1660 through the 1670s has to be deduced from scattered references mainly in poems and plays, and there is little agreement as to what they mean. But the evidence available, though slight, is by no means unimportant. What we know about Dryden's family background in particular indicates with virtual certainty the general nature of his religious affiliation before the Restoration. This, together with certain facts we have about his university education, may be used to shed needed light on the religious opinions expressed in the poems, plays, and assorted prose works he wrote between 1660 and the late 1670s. Indeed, a reexamination of the question of Dryden's early religious thought may reveal a good deal.

Dryden very rarely referred in his writings to the early parts of his life. Probably the most important of these references is the well-known *confessio* in the First Part of *The Hind and the Panther*, in which he describes his different intellectual positions before conversion:

My thoughtless youth was wing'd with vain desires,
My manhood, long misled by wandring fires,
Follow'd false lights; and when their glimps was gone,
My pride struck out new sparkles of her own.

(ll. 72–75)

Scott believed that by the "vain desires" of his "thoughtless youth" Dryden meant "that inattention to religious duties which the amusements of youth too frequently occasion. The 'false lights' which bewildered the poet's manhood were, I doubt not, the puritanical tenets, which . . . he must have at least professed, but probably seriously entertained." [1] Whether this interpretation of Dryden's lines is correct, there can be no doubt that his background was Puritan. Though there is reason to doubt that he was "A Bristled *Baptist* bred," as his enemies frequently claimed,[2] his relations, maternal and paternal, were staunchly Puritan. Scott describes the poet's grandfathers as both "fanatics." [3] More important, his father Erasmus, according to the poet's early biographer Edmund Malone, served as "Justice of Peace and Committee-man, in the county of Northampton during the Usurpation, and was a zealous presbyterian." [4] Erasmus's brother John, for whom the poet may have been named, was, we are told, "a flaming and bigoted puritan." [5] Of course, when Dryden was growing up, Puritanism was all about him. He cannot, therefore, have escaped Puritan influence. [6]

About the shape of Dryden's beliefs as a Puritan we can say little. At least in terms of later effects, however, the nature of our information concerning his relatives is important and probably indicates a good deal about his own earliest views. Much of what we know about the Drydens and the Pickerings concerns their antiprelaticism and anticlericalism. Sir Erasmus Dryden, the poet's grandfather, was arrested in 1604 and imprisoned for circulating a petition on behalf of Puritan ministers. He continued, however, to defend the preachers and became a patron of the Puritan divine John Dod, who was "silenced" by Archbishop Abbot in 1611. [7] On the other side of the family Lewis Pickering, great-uncle of the poet's cousin-german Sir Gilbert and a man notorious for his Puritan zeal, may have written a scandalous verse libel on Archbishops Whitgift and Bancroft.[8] Such beliefs were passed on. We can easily imagine that the poet's father shared them; he had, after all, attended Emmanuel College, Cambridge, which proclaimed its Calvinistic sympathies and where the education was "circumspectly anti-prelatical."[9] About the poet's uncle John there can be no doubt. According to contemporary accounts he "was very furious against the clergy," and Malone reports that he "desecrated" the church at Canons Ashby, which he then possessed.[10] Thus, as Dryden's recent biographer supposes, the poet must have been introduced very early to conversations centering on "the 'unreasonable' edicts of the bishops."[11] Of importance too is Dryden's apparently close relationship to his cousin, the rabid and influential Sir Gilbert Pickering. The poet may have been in Sir Gilbert's employ in the late 1650s when the latter was Oliver Cromwell's Lord Chamberlain; certainly he was in his company in London. Sir Gilbert was, we are told, "first a presbyterian, then an independent, then a Brownist, and afterwards an anabaptist. He was a most furious, fiery, implacable man; was the principal agent in casting out most of the learned clergy; a great oppressor of the country."[12] We may safely assume that the anticlericalism so prominently displayed in Dryden's own works throughout his life had its beginnings in this period.

Dryden's experiences at Trinity College, Cambridge, which he attended from 1650 to 1654, are not likely to have changed substantially his puritanical and anticlerical opinions. If, as many believe, the new science derived considerable strength from Puritanism, then the nature of his university education may actually have complemented and supported earlier influences. At any rate, according to Seth Ward, writing in 1654, the new science was flourishing at both Oxford and Cambridge, an assessment that the work of recent scholars confirms.[13] That Dryden was enrolled in Trinity is itself significant, for Trinity "was the most important outpost of the new science at Cambridge,"[14] occupying a place analogous to that of Wadham College at Oxford, out of which the Royal Society grew. Bacon had attended Trinity, whose character in the middle of the seventeenth century is suggested by the fact that John Wilkins, one of the prime movers behind the foundation of the Royal Society, left Wadham to become its master and that Isaac Newton enrolled there in 1661. Among Dryden's fellow students, in fact, were a number of future scientists and Fellows of the Society, including the physicians Thomas Allen and John Mapletoft, the embryologist Walter Needham, and the zoologist Francis Willughby. I do not mean to suggest that Dryden received a scientific education at Trinity, but surely he was introduced to lively conversations about experiments, the nature of the pioneering work being done, and the hopes and plans for the future. More important perhaps for a nonscientist was the assault on intellectual dogma and authority that all students watched and that a great many contributed to. The attitudes of dissent from the Ancients and "the ideals of freedom of inquiry and of cautious diffidence bequeathed by Bacon were as much a part of the contribution Trinity College made to the new science as were the experiments conducted in the chambers of some of its members." [15] The universities fostered the new philosophy, therefore, not only by training the scientists but also by "helping to create an intellectual class which could encourage and support the work of genius." [16]

The effort was not wasted on Dryden. He was for a while a member in good standing of the Royal Society and a friend of such Society figures as Walter Charleton and Thomas Sprat, its official historian. Dryden's celebrated skepticism appears a reflection of the scientists' own mode of open inquiry. Certainly, his hearty endorsement of the methods, aims, and aspirations of the scientists, which testifies to the success of his education at Trinity, appears prominently in the poems and criticism he wrote during the 1660s and early 1670s. Dryden's relation to the new science, as expressed in these works, establishes the pattern of his early thinking and so bears directly on the question of his religious opinions.

One of the best known of Dryden's statements on the new

science is "To My Honored Friend, Dr. Charleton." Like Bacon who charged that reverence for ancient authorities kept men back from progress in the sciences, Dryden begins by attacking the tyranny of Aristotelianism and proceeds to the praise of advance and modern superiority frequently heard at the time. He then specifically praises several who have contributed to the march of scientific progress, beginning with Bacon, who, Cowley later wrote, "chac'd ['Autority'] out of our sight." [17] Dryden goes on to list the achievements of Gilbert, the brothers Boyle, Harvey, and George Ent, concluding with Charleton, who shares with the more illustrious figures "that initial scepticism of a received opinion which leads to a new discovery." [18]

The attitudes expressed in this poem reappear in the critical prose of the 1660s and 1670s in what has been called Dryden's "conscious self-projection as a modernist." [19] Perhaps the best known of these scattered remarks is in *Of Dramatic Poesy: An Essay*. That the speaker at this point is Crites, who elsewhere urges the preeminence of the Ancients in the arts, attests to the prevalence of the new optimism in the Restoration. Crites's rejection of Aristotle's authority and praise of scientific method, alongside a sense of the present as enlightened and thus distinct from a scientifically ignorant past, echoes the celebrated fulminations of Bacon, Sprat, and others. "Is it not evident," Crites asks, "in these last hundred years (when the study of philosophy has been the business of all the virtuosi in Christendom), that almost a new nature has been revealed to us? that more errors of the school have been detected, more useful experiments in philosophy have been made, more noble secrets in optics, medicine, anatomy, astronomy discovered, than in all those credulous and doting ages from Aristotle to us? so true it is, that nothing spreads more fast than science, when rightly and generally cultivated." [20] Crites's reference to "a new nature" suggests his (and Dryden's) agreement with Hakewill in the famous controversy with Goodman concerning the decay of the earth following the Fall. It suggests as well the more mechanical conception of the universe described by the scientists, rather than

the centuries-old awareness of nature as the visible manifestation of God's presence in his created effects. In the dramatic arts,
moreover, the *Essay* posits a definite progress.

Elsewhere Dryden pursues the attack on the tyranny of authority, said by the Moderns to have prevented progress. In the
Preface to *An Evening's Love* (1671), for example, he deplores the
tendency in criticism to exalt Jonson as an authority and to per-
mit no questioning of him. "I know I have been accused as an
enemy of [Jonson's] writings; but without any other reason than
that I do not admire him blindly, and without looking into his
imperfections. For why should he only be exempted from those
frailties from which Homer and Virgil are not free? Or why
should there be any *ipse dixit* in our poetry, any more than there
is in our philosophy?"[21] Explicated by Simon Patrick in *A Brief
Account of the New Sect of Latitude-Men*, the attitude is entirely familiar. As one recent commentator has noted, citing lines from
the poem to Dr. Charleton, "To reverence Jonson as an authority
in the drama whose theory and practice of comedy must be 'ad-
mired blindly' is to pay 'that homage to a *Name*, / Which onely
God and *Nature* justly claim.' *Nullius in verba* is a motto to which
poets have as much right as the members of the Royal Society."[22] That right Dryden exercised the following year in his
"Defence of the Epilogue: or An Essay on the Dramatic Poetry of
the Last Age," in which he declined to yield to the authority of
Shakespeare and Fletcher as well as of Jonson and the older
dramatists.

> I would ascribe to dead authors their just praises in those
> things wherein they have excelled us; and in those where-
> in we contend with them for the pre-eminence, I would ac-
> knowledge our advantages to the age, and claim no victory
> from our wit. This being what I have proposed to myself, I
> hope I shall not be thought arrogant when I inquire into
> their errors. For we live in an age so sceptical, that as it de-
> termines little, so it takes nothing from antiquity on trust.
> And I profess to have no other ambition in this essay than

that poetry may not go backward, when all arts and sciences are advancing.[23]

Dryden's modernism is restrained, certainly not extreme. It is his emphasis, the main direction of his thought, that I am trying to establish.

Of the works which bear on the nature of Dryden's early involvement with the new science none is more important than *Annus Mirabilis* (1667), with its "Apostrophe to the Royal Society."[24] This section is preceded by a "Digression concerning Shipping and Navigation," which concludes with a grand utopian vision that comprehends the entire earth:

> Instructed ships shall sail to quick Commerce;
>   By which remotest Regions are alli'd:
> Which makes one City of the Universe,
>   Where some may gain, and all may be suppli'd.
>
> Then, we upon our Globes last verge shall go,
>   And view the Ocean leaning on the sky:
> From thence our rolling Neighbours we shall know,
>   And on the Lunar world securely pry.
>
> (ll. 649-56)

This possibility is predicated, as the "Apostrophe" establishes, on English success in acquiring knowledge and learning to control nature:

> This I fore-tel, from your auspicious care,
>   Who great in search of God and Nature grow:
> Who best your wise Creator's praise declare,
>   Since best to praise his works is best to know.
>
> O truly Royal! who behold the Law,
>   And rule of beings in your Makers mind,
> And thence, like Limbecks, rich Idea's draw,
>   To fit the levell'd use of humane kind.
>
> (ll. 657–64)

As Michael McKeon observes, "The wonder of this distinctively urban Eden is that universal peace and plenty will be re-created, in a world grown unimaginably complex, not by teaching humans to temper their sinful and selfish desires but by regulating nature to accommodate those desires to the fullest extent."[25]

The direction of Dryden's thought in *Annus Mirabilis* has been helpfully analyzed by McKeon, who corrects a number of misconceptions regarding the poem and its procedures, including widespread notions concerning its eschatological elements. According to McKeon, "what Dryden discredits is not the peculiarly dissenting *habit* of prophecy and eschatology, but the peculiarly dissenting *policies* which this virtually universal habit may be used to advocate." McKeon demonstrates the prevalence of this "habit" in Royalists, whose messianism was as great as the republicans', though ideologically different. Thus "if Fifth Monarchy Men envisioned the universal reign of Christ and his saints upon earth, Charles's supporters frequently looked for a magnificent era of imperialism—martial, commercial, and religious—inaugurated by Charles as the instrument or vicegerent of Christ." At least as important for our purposes here are the implications McKeon draws out of Dryden's faith in and allegiance to scientific method. He correctly observes, for instance, that scientific method is "rigorously individualistic" and that "the empirical premises of the new science are totally subversive of authoritarianism in the realm of natural knowledge and, by necessary implication, in the realm of received political and socioeconomic wisdom as well." He concludes: "Because it is so closely identified with scientific method in *Annus Mirabilis*, Dryden's bold liberty of prophesying is far bolder than he intends. It prepares not for the renovation of prelapsarian absolutism and 'reasons of state,' but for the ascendancy of individualism and the commonplace invocation of 'individual rights' in all spheres of public life."[26] If Dryden did not comprehend the implications of his position in *Annus Mirabilis,* he understood them fully by the 1680s.

What emerges from *Annus Mirabilis* and the other works we have noted is a picture of Dryden in the first decade and a half of the Restoration as enlightened and committed to the attitudes of the new science and little inclined to accept opinions on authority, insistent on individual freedom, trusting in the power of man and especially his technology, and optimistic about the future promised by the increase of man's knowledge and his seemingly inevitable control of physical nature. Flushed with the prospects for progress and plenty opened up by Baconianism, prospects strengthened by the return of a king who chartered the Royal Society, Dryden seems not to have had then what Burke called "the moral imagination." In this period of his life Dryden shows little awareness that in the way of progress and an eventual utopia stands the complex and imperfectible nature of man himself, rather than simply ignorance, superstition, and material encumbrances.[27] His eye is on the future, the past often appearing hardly more than a dark age from which the present has happily evolved.

What this tells us about Dryden's religious thought at the time is quite a lot. The freedom of inquiry likely affected his thinking on religious matters in a profound way. Certainly the religious thinking of others in the Restoration who embraced the antiauthoritarianism and empirical ideals of the new science, such as Wilkins, More, Sprat, and Glanvill, reveals a complementarily liberal quality; in contrast, the more religiously conservative Robert South, for example, disparaged the new science. There is no substantive evidence I know of to suggest that Dryden or any other of these men was then or ever a free-thinker. Whether or not Dryden changed his religious as well as his political affiliation upon Charles's return, he evidently became an Anglican sometime in the early years of his reign. In some sense he seems to have been of that kind known as Latitudinarian. As has been frequently noted, the Latitudinarian theologians undertook a "*rapprochement* with the new thought," embracing the procedures and attitudes of the scientists.[28] What they accomplished, along with the Cambridge Platonists and the founders of the Royal Society, was "a new mentality"[29]— like the "mind" Dryden displays in the works of the 1660s and early 1670s. Christian to be sure, and not tainted with Deism, as often charged, this religious thinking is nevertheless clearly distinct from the traditionalism and emphatic Augustinianism of Catholics and such High Church Anglicans as George Hickes.

Other evidence is available regarding Dryden's religious opinions in the 1660s and 1670s. Frequently cited by commentators is the scene in *Tyrannick Love* where Saint Catherine attempts to convert the heathen philosopher Apollonius by means of rational argument. Catherine begins by asserting that whereas "our Reason with our Faith does go," "Reason with your fond Religion fights" (II.i.169, 171).[30] When Apollonius, forced into the dispute by the ranting emperor Maximin, defends the "solid truths" that lie in "precepts of Morality," Catherine confronts precisely those "Rules." She argues first the difficulty in following the "strict" rules given by philosophy and then the advantage of Christianity in promising rewards for virtuous acts. To this, Apollonius responds: "By how much more your Faith reward assures, / So much more frank our Virtue is than yours" (203–4). Catherine claims, however, that the pagans too seek the rewards that Apollonius damns. The issue becomes, then, the nature of the rewards. Weakened, Apollonius maintains now that Christians obey "our Moral Virtues." Catherine's response follows, defeating her opponent:

> *S. Cath.* 'Tis true, your virtues are the same we teach;
> But in our practice they much higher reach.
> You but forbid to take anothers due;
> But we forbid ev'n to desire it too.
> Revenge of injuries you Virtue call;
> But we forgiveness of our wrongs extoll:
> Immodest deeds you hinder to be wrought,
> But we proscribe the least immodest thought.
> So much your Virtues are in ours refin'd,
> That yours but reach the actions, ours the mind.
>   *Max.* Answer in short to what you heard her speak.
> [*To Apol.*]
>   *Apol.* Where Truth prevails, all arguments are weak.

To that convincing power I must give place:
And with that Truth, that Faith I will embrace.
$$(211-24)$$

Because Dryden provides Catherine with arguments based solely on the rational and ethical superiority of Christianity and
omits all mention of religious authority, grace, and even God,
some scholars align him with rationalism, even Deism. But Dryden's limitation here can be accounted for dramatically. Catherine argues the ethical superiority of her religion because those
are the terms in which Apollonius wants to argue. When she
overcomes the objections he thought unanswerable, he must
yield. The limitation thus leads to an effective dramatic revelation of the superiority of the Christian religion. Clearly, however, Catherine's is an enlightened faith, speeches like the
following recalling the "Anglican rationalists" as well as the reasonableness of the layman's faiths:

Thus, with short Plummets Heav'ns deep will we sound,
That vast Abyss where humane Wit is drown'd!
In our small Skiff we must not launce too far;
We here but Coasters, not Discov'rers are.
Faith's necessary Rules are plain and few;
We, many, and those needless Rules pursue:
Faith from our hearts into our heads we drive;
And make Religion all Contemplative.
You, on Heav'ns will may witty glosses feign;
But that which I must practise here, is plain.
$$(IV.i.544-53)$$

Because Dryden's position remained relatively unchanged
for some time, *The Indian Emperour,* published three years before
Tyrannick Love, will clarify the nature of Dryden's enlightened
attitudes. Often cited in the scholarship on Dryden's thought is
the discussion of the merits of Christianity in Act Five, a passage

similar to that in the later play. In this discussion between a corrupt Spanish priest and the "noble savage" Montezuma and his High Priest, both of whom are being stretched on the rack, Dryden again forgoes any appeal to revelation, this time evincing seemingly more attraction for the natural religion described by the emperor. This has led Pierre Legouis to characterize Montezuma as "n'est plus l'empéreur aztèque, c'est un déiste anglais du xviie siècle," and Bredvold similarly has said that the "argument of Montezuma certainly comes near to being Deism."[31] The discussion begins with the points of agreement between Christians and pagans. Differences soon appear: Montezuma declares, "Where both agree 'tis there most safe to stay: / For what's more vain then Publick Light to shun, / And set up Tapers while we see the Sun?" (V.ii.68–70). The priest responds that, though nature teaches men to adore God, "Heavenly Beams" tell much more. Montezuma's reply leads to the climax of the discussion:

> *Mont.* Or this must be enough, or to Mankind
> One equal way to Bliss is not design'd.
> For though some more may know, and some know less,
> Yet all must know enough for happiness.
> *Chr. Pr.* If in this middle way you still pretend
> To stay, your Journey never will have end.
> *Mont.* Howe're, 'tis better in the midst to stay,
> Then wander farther in uncertain way.
> *Chr. Pr.* But we by Martyrdom our Faith avow.
> *Mont.* You do no more then I for ours do now.
> To prove Religion true——
> If either Wit or Suff'rings would suffice,
> All Faiths afford the Constant and the Wise:
> And yet ev'n they, by Education sway'd,
> In Age defend what Infancy obey'd.
> *Chr. Pr.* Since Age by erring Child-hood is misled,
> Refer your self to our Un-erring Head.
> *Mont.* Man and not erre! what reason can you give?
> *Chr. Pr.* Renounce that carnal reason, and believe.

> *Mont.* The Light of Nature should I thus betray,
> 'Twere to wink hard that I might see the day.
> 　*Chr. Pr.* Condemn not yet the way you do not know;
> I'le make your reason judge what way to go.
> 　*Mont.* 'Tis much too late for me new ways to take,
> Who have but one short step of life to make.
> 　*Piz.* Increase their Pains, the Cords are yet too slack.
> 　*Chr. Pr.* I must by force, convert him on the Rack.
> 　　　　　　　　　　　　　　　　　(73–99)

Many of the ideas here, as well as the phrasing and imagery, anticipate, as do Catherine's remarks, *Religio Laici* many years later, though Dryden's understanding then of the necessary "middle way" is quite different from Montezuma's here. Dryden's own position in the mid-1660s is not so easy to determine. It is by no means certain that Montezuma speaks for Dryden; he is not a normative character.

I would suggest that *The Indian Emperour* reflects not so much an inclination on Dryden's part toward Montezuma's principles of natural religion as a sympathetic interpretation of his position as noble and dignified. One need only compare Dryden's presentation of the Deist in *Religio Laici* (depicted as foolishly proud and as a "poor Worm") to appreciate how much Dryden changed by 1682; though in that later work he could only criticize the Deist, fifteen years earlier he could at least sympathize with him. Moreover, rather than stressing the virtues of natural religion, *The Indian Emperour* focuses on the hypocritical practice of Christians; Montezuma's intransigence is at least partly attributable to the corruption he witnesses in the Spaniards. It is the example set particularly by the Catholic priesthood, proudly authoritarian, indeed tyrannical, greedy, and insensitive, that Dryden blasts, not Christianity itself. This criticism is unsparing, and it is important to note that Dryden directs it, not at the wicked nature of man, but at the institution his character represents.[32] I cannot agree with Budick, then, that Dryden was "in some sense, deistic in the earlier part of his career."[33]

Of the play's corrupt Spaniards, easily the most hypocritical and the least merciful is the Christian priest. The priest tortures Montezuma on the rack in a vain effort both to convert him and to wring from him the whereabouts of his stores of gold. In denouncing the priest's action the Spanish leader Cortez underscores its heinousness: "What dismal sight is this, which takes from me / All the delight that waits on Victory!" (113–14).

Dryden is critical of the priesthood because he recognizes the clergy's great importance as exemplars of the Christian religion and wants it free of such contamination as helps confirm Montezuma in his choice of natural religion; from the beginning through "The Character of a Good Parson," included in the *Fables* (1700), Dryden insisted that the priesthood must set an example of the Christian faith. Dryden wanted the priesthood free of temporal aspirations as well. Montezuma says here, probably speaking for Dryden, "He who Religion truely understands / Knows its extent must be in Men, not Lands" (I.ii.297–98). Indeed, Dryden insists that, if allowed to participate in affairs of state, the priesthood by its very nature will pose serious threats to monarchy. According to Pizarro, "though the Royal Dignity they own, / [Priests] Are equal to it, and depend on none" (311–12); to this Guyomar replies, "Depend on none! you treat them sure in state, / For 'tis their plenty does their pride create" (313–14). Montezuma then declares:

> Those ghostly Kings would parcel out my pow'r,
> And all the fatness of my Land devour;
> That Monarch sits not safely on his Throne,
> Who suffers any pow'r, to shock his own.
> They teach obedience to Imperial sway,
> But think it sin if they themselves obey.
>
> (315–20)

Echoing these views later on, Cortez is quite blunt:

> [*To the Chr. Priest*]
> And you, ———
> Who sawcily, teach Monarchs to obey,

And the wide World in narrow Cloysters sway;
Set up by Kings as humble aids of power,
You that which bred you, Viper-like devour,
You Enemies of Crowns————

(V.ii.125–30)

The fourth line here smacks of Hobbism and may or may not represent Dryden's own position. In any case, as glimpsed in the remarks he gave to Montezuma and Cortez, Dryden was committed to the supremacy of the crown in state affairs, opposed to clerical involvement in politics and other matters secular, insistent that churchmen confine their teaching and personal involvement to the spiritual. Probably deriving from his Puritan background,[34] this desire for a clergy "purified" of worldly interests is a consistent theme in Dryden and appears whenever he treats of churchmen. Early on it seems part of a merely fashionable attack on Catholicism, Puritanism, and hypocrisy in general, favorite targets of the wits and Restoration dramatists, rather than the expression of a concern of great importance to Dryden. Later it deepens, and toward the end of his career, in *Don Sebastian* and the "Good Parson," especially, it forms the basis of his opposition to *de jure* Anglican priests.

In the early works a satirical interest in correcting clerical abuse characterizes his frequent attacks on priestly self-interest, particularly greed and hypocrisy. Though Dryden often used the Roman Catholic clergy as his vehicle, as in *The Indian Emperour* and *The Assignation: or, Love in a Nunnery* (1673), his criticism is not limited to that priesthood. In *Astraea Redux* (1660), for example, after condemning the recent expulsion of the Anglican clergy and the confiscation of their chapels, Dryden levels these charges against Puritan ministers:

Religions name against it self was made;
The shadow serv'd the substance to invade:
Like Zealous Missions they did care pretend
Of souls in shew, but made the Gold their end.

(ll. 191–94)

In his first play, *The Wild Gallant* (1663), the clergy generally are
said to be masters of intrigue, designed for self-aggrandizement:
"betwixt [the devil and churchmen] there must be Warr: yet to
do u'm both right, I think in my conscience they quarrel onely
like Lawyers; for their Fees; and meet good friends in private to
laugh at their Clients" (V.iv.13–16). Similar statements occur
elsewhere in the play, as well as in *The Conquest of Granada*. Dryden finds the clergy's lust for gold and debasement of their function so widespread and familiar that he can use it as a simile in
Annus Mirabilis:

> Our greedy Sea-men rummage every hold,
>   Smile on the booty of each wealthier Chest:
> And, as the Priests who with their gods make bold,
>   Take what they like, and sacrifice the rest.[35]
>
>   (ll. 829–32)

Such comments, which increase markedly in both frequency
and intensity beginning in the late 1670s, are scattered throughout the plays, poems, and critical works Dryden wrote in the
first decade and a half of the Restoration; I have provided only a
representative selection.

   Probably strengthened by the antiauthoritarianism of the empirical attitude he adopted, as well as by the character of the
age,[36] Dryden's anticlericalism is an important element in the
pattern of thought I have described as enlightened. Taking into
account both his opposition to priests and his "conscious self-
projection as a modernist," it appears that Dryden's early thinking, while Christian, resembles the position of the layman's faiths
more than the Latitudinarianism of Anglican divines, both of
which reflect the forward-looking attitudes of the new science.

   If Dryden's religious position from 1660 to the late 1670s is
enlightened Christianity, rather than Deism or free-thinking, it
is still not entirely secure in its beliefs. I should like in conclusion
to emphasize with reference to the heroic dramas the tension
that exists in this period between Dryden's basic allegiance to
the Christian view and the assertive individualism that we have

seen to be implicit in his thinking and certainly explicit in his age, including in areas that affected him profoundly. Anne T. Barbeau has recently argued that Divine Justice is "the central agent" in these plays as well as in the early "heroic" poems; Dryden, she maintains, shows that "history is not in the hands of men but is the working out of a preordained plan which will providentially bring about the instauration of peace and justice on earth."[37] This, I think, requires qualification. Though Barbeau is right to insist that *The Conquest of Granada*, for example, is structured in such a way as to demonstrate the eventual triumph of Divine Justice, whatever particular men may do, it is also true that Almanzor's heroic individualism, which leads to several changes in political allegiance as well as to the claim that "I alone am king of me" (Part One, I.i.), is intensely focused and made dramatically attractive. That the plays support this individualism, though not the naturalism, Hobbism, epicureanism, or Machiavellianism of the various villains, is indicated by the fact that—to refer only to *The Conquest of Granada*—Almanzor is a noble and ennobling figure, positively influencing Almahide, who is sometimes mistakenly thought to be the instrument of his education and socialization, and that he agrees to accept Spanish society at the end because he has found in Ferdinand a kindred spirit, that is, the kind of "haughty mind" that insists as he does on virtue, purity, and excellence. Though the hero's willful self-assertion is mitigated by play's end, as he is reconciled to society in the triumph of Divine Justice, it is that "haughty mind" and the greatness of soul he shares with the other heroes that receives the attention and that the reader specially recalls.

That Dryden later repudiated such individualism may be seen if one compares the description of Almanzor with the similar one of Achitophel written nine years later. The later figure is introduced—and condemned—as

> A fiery Soul, which working out its way,
> Fretted the Pigmy Body to decay:
> And o'r inform'd the Tenement of Clay.

3

Dryden's Religious Views 1677–1684

When we turn from a reading of the works Dryden wrote in the 1660s and early and mid-1670s to *Mac Flecknoe, Absalom and Achitophel, The Medall,* and *Religio Laici,* we are struck at once by the differences in his understanding. Evidently a major intellectual conversion had occurred, no doubt induced in part by a growing awareness of the ramifications of the new thought.[1] Whenever and for whatever specific reasons it came about, it produced in Dryden a new insistence on the primacy of the moral in literary invention and on the moral function of poetry.[2] It also led to his greatest literary achievements. I shall try here to describe the nature of Dryden's change in understanding as reflected in the poems (excluding *Religio Laici*), plays, and prose works written between 1677 and his conversion to Roman Catholicism. A major failure of commentary on Dryden's religious thinking has been the almost total neglect of the works I discuss in this chapter.

Published in 1682 but almost certainly composed by 1678, *Mac Flecknoe* is one of the first works to reflect Dryden's new outlook. As a satire it represents a new departure for Dryden. Prior to the late 1670s, possessing a tolerant, even optimistic view of man and believing in the inevitability of progress, he was more likely to praise than to blame.[3] When he did ridicule, the abuse was mainly *à la mode* and aimed at the institutions the witty and enlightened thought to be in need of their lashes for old-fashioned, tyrannical, and hypocritical beliefs and actions. Beginning around the time of *Mac Flecknoe,* however, the satire is directed not haphazardly at obvious targets, but at particular and immediate situations generated by the vices and follies of individual men. Dryden's concerns are indeed more moral than before, for he now seems better to understand man's wicked heart.

If in moving from the early and exuberant Charleton poem and *Annus Mirabilis* to *Mac Flecknoe* praise has become satire, the prospect of immediate and unlimited progress has been transformed into a vision of unrelieved decay. The pervasive sense of absolute ruin, apparent from the opening line ("All humane things are subject to decay") to the scatological "subterranean wind" at the close, may be best illustrated with reference to the important account of the Nursery. What appears to be merely a spatial description turns out on closer examination to be an image of the process of historical decay.

> Close to the Walls which fair *Augusta* bind,
> (The fair *Augusta* much to fears inclin'd)
> An ancient fabrick, rais'd t' inform the sight,
> There stood of yore, and *Barbican* it hight:
> A watch Tower once; but now, so Fate ordains,
> Of all the Pile an empty name remains.
> From its old Ruins Brothel-houses rise,
> Scenes of lewd loves, and of polluted joys;
> Where their vast Courts the Mother-Strumpets keep,
> And, undisturb'd by Watch, in silence sleep.
> Near these a Nursery erects its head,
> Where Queens are form'd, and future Hero's bred;
> Where unfledg'd Actors learn to laugh and cry, ⎫
> Where infant Punks their tender Voices try, ⎬
> And little *Maximins* the Gods defy. ⎭
> Great *Fletcher* never treads in Buskins here,
> Nor greater *Johnson* dares in Socks appear.
> But gentle *Simkin* just reception finds

Amidst this Monument of vanisht minds:
Pure Clinches, the suburbian Muse affords;
And *Panton* waging harmless War with words.
Here *Fleckno,* as a place to Fame well known,
Ambitiously design'd his *Sh*——'s Throne.

(ll. 64–86)

Behind this description of the Nursery stands the well-known seventeenth-century tradition of eulogizing "a great public monument for its embodiment and continuation of tradition."[4] But whereas the structures described in Jonson's "To Penshurst" and Marvell's *Upon Appleton House,* for example, point to the accumulated wisdom of mankind in bodying forth a magnificent order, Shadwell's coronation place is a "Monument of vanisht minds" and so represents absence instead of living presence. As Edward Pechter shrewdly observes, "The dream of the new science, sprung from Bacon's progressivist hopes, turns here into nightmare. Rather than legitimately extending tradition by refining it, the Nursery represents a radical alienation from all the values of the past."[5]

It would be a mistake, I think, to conclude that Dryden's gloom results simply from disappointment over crushed hopes, now that the promise of the early years of Charles's reign has ushered in bourgeois mediocrity. The reasons for the pessimism of *Mac Flecknoe* cut much deeper. If the present is fallen, the decline is measured not by the halcyon days of the early 1660s, but rather by the standards of traditional understanding formerly supported by art but now subverted. Moreover, ancient wisdom looms impressively, and in particular Dryden's view of the Ancients and the nature they "read" differs from the sanguine picture of "a new nature" he extolled a few years earlier. His optimistic faith in Moderns diminished, he now offers a new estimation of the Ancients in the Preface to *All for Love,* where he calls them "our masters," and in "The Grounds of Criticism in Tragedy," prefixed to *Troilus and Cressida* (1679), which contrasts vividly with the position taken in *Of Dramatic Poesy: An Essay;* here he advises imitation of Shakespeare and Fletcher "so far only as they have copied the excellencies of those who invented and brought to perfection dramatic poetry."⁶ As Dryden put it in the dedication of *Plutarch's Lives* (1683) in "powerful periods that roll over the reader like tidal waves" and that constitute "one of the most fervent manifestos in English literature for believers in a golden age of the past and one of the most magnificent admissions of individual and corporate inferiority in his contemporary world":

> Not only the Bodies, but the Souls of Men, have decreas'd from the vigour of the first Ages; . . . we are not more short of the stature and strength of those gygantick Heroes, than we are of their understanding, and their wit.
> . . . How vast a difference is there betwixt the productions of those Souls, and these of ours! How much better *Plato*, *Aristotle*, and the rest of the Philosophers understood nature; *Thucydides*, and *Herodotus* adorn'd History; *Sophocles*, *Euripides* and *Menander* advanc'd Poetry, than those Dwarfs of Wit and Learning who succeeded them in after times!⁷

Without neglecting the Puritan and Whiggish background of the city, its crass materialism and its unruly mobs,⁸ Dryden focuses on the deterioration of art in the hands of the poets the city prefers and the loss of understanding that results from that decay. Opposed to the impulse toward earthy realism and the naturalistic in poets like Shadwell, Dryden insists that literature reflect "perfect nature."⁹ What Shadwell provides is not Nature but a severely limited and distorted approximation, a parody, void of presence, not altogether different perhaps from the "new nature" drawn by the scientists. "What share have we in Nature or in Art?" asks Flecknoe (l. 176), innocent of the key terms' meaning. Dryden's reiterated conflation of distinct kinds of reality in the poem is evidently intended to dramatize Shadwell's confusion of art with life naturalistically interpreted and his ultimate reduction of both to one dead level. In the final six lines, of course, characters from *Psyche* step out of the play to effect Flecknoe's departure and to enthrone their author.

Shadwell's failure to transform life into art leads inexorably in those who absorb his work to the same leveling of sensibility and deadening of consciousness that he represents so well. Nowhere is the significance of Shadwell's dullness clearer than in the remarks on wit:

> Some Beams of Wit on other souls may fall,
> Strike through and make a lucid interval;
> But *Sh*——'s genuine night admits no ray,
> His rising Fogs prevail upon the Day.
>
> (ll. 21–24)

Drawing on the ancient tradition which equates light with Being and darkness with nonbeing, Dryden carefully establishes the consequences of Shadwell's parody of art. "Born for a scourge of wit, and flayle of Sense" (l. 89), Shadwell must swear "Ne'er to have peace with Wit, nor truce with Sense" (l. 117). Instead he is to "wage immortal War with Wit" (l. 12) and thus destroy the human faculty which can perceive the physical creation as not wholly material but potentially intelligible as "the manifestation . . . of the Order and Reason behind all things, a reflection of the medieval view that the likeness of God is implanted in the very matter and organization of the universe."[10] Unaware that everything is itself and at the same time a reflection of something more than itself, Shadwell's realism can only celebrate things for what they seem, not for what they mean.

The effects of the spread of dullness are, of course, already observable in the world of the poem. Partly as a result of the penchant for "tortur[ing] one poor word Ten thousand ways" (l. 208) and so "waging harmless War with words" (l. 84), "vanisht minds" are everywhere. Instead of reflecting the light visible in Nature, heightening consciousness, and fulfilling the poet's responsibilities as caretaker of language, tradition, and morality, Shadwell will create "Some peacefull Province in Acrostick Land" (l. 206). Like Flecknoe, "flourishing in Peace" (l. 7), Shadwell will secure accommodation with human nature, rather than encourage discipline, control, and the correction of follies and

vices. For as Flecknoe proudly proclaims, asserting the importance of gentleness:

> Like mine thy gentle numbers feebly creep,
> Thy Tragick Muse gives smiles, thy Comick sleep.
> With whate'er gall thou sett'st thy self to write,
> Thy inoffensive Satyrs never bite.
>
> (ll. 197–200)

Dryden aptly summarizes Shadwell's perversion of the poet's
public responsibility in comparing "the hopefull boy" (l. 61) with
Hannibal, sworn enemy of Rome:

> The hoary Prince in Majesty appear'd,
> High on a Throne of his own Labours rear'd.
> At his right hand our young *Ascanius* sate,
> *Rome*'s other hope, and pillar of the State.
> His Brows thick fogs, instead of glories, grace,
> And lambent dullness plaid around his face.
> As *Hannibal* did to the Altars come,
> Sworn by his *Syre* a mortal Foe to *Rome;*
> So *Sh*—— swore, nor should his Vow bee vain,
> That he till Death true dullness would maintain;
> And in his father's Right, and Realms defence,
> Ne'er to have peace with Wit, nor truce with Sense.
>
> (ll. 106–17)

As the frequent political references and analogies suggest, Dryden is drawing too on the tradition in which "the law-giver is
. . . named beside the poet, and the formulas which define the
law beside the wise utterances of the poet." [11]

The civil and religious functions of the poet, as Dryden images them, may finally be inseparable. For if, as Sanford Budick
has recently argued, [12] Dryden, like Milton before and Pope and
Johnson afterwards, accepted the biblical notion of the poet as
keryx, the true poet may be a prophet, that is, one who speaks
for God and who has been chosen in some sense to lead his peo-

ple. Though the several references in the poem to prophets and prophecy have usually been interpreted as simply another strike at Flecknoe and Shadwell, particularly as they are linked to Dissenting attitudes, Dryden may not be reviling at all the idea of the poet's prophetic function but rather the parody of that idea by bad poets. Given the evident foundation of *Annus Mirabilis* in prophecy, this seems plausible.

Not unrelated, I believe, is the fact that beginning in 1678 Dryden increasingly scored the clergy for failing to adhere to their duties and responsibilities. From *Troilus and Cressida* (1679) through *The Duke of Guise* (1683) Dryden's works, dramatic and nondramatic, may be seen as attempting to fulfill at least part of the function traditionally performed by churchmen but now being neglected. *Religio Laici* is the culmination of this effort to supplement and correct those who, like Shadwell, fail to do the necessary work of maintaining access to Being itself. The particular way in which Dryden now treats the clergy is one manifestation of his increasing interest in matters religious and spiritual, which exists alongside growing doubts regarding the world and especially the realm of politics.

For whatever reasons, Dryden's antipathy toward priests increased markedly in the late 1670s, and for the next several years he treated them with a violence unmatched even in an era of anticlericalism.[13] Jeremy Collier's outraged cry that "the English *Oedipus* makes the Priesthood an Imposturous Profession, and rails at the whole Order"[14] contains more truth than one likely expects. For during these years, invoking the concept anathematized by churchmen, Dryden wastes few opportunities to expose *priestcraft*. In his treatment that term, so often used by Deists and free-thinkers, is defined as a failure to adhere to the spiritual function, resulting from a self-interested desire for money, place, and power that has led to various forms of worldly engagement, including political intrigue. Maintaining that "Priests of all Religions are the same" (l. 99), Dryden begins *Absalom and Achitophel* by insinuating that priestcraft makes piety virtually impossible (l. 1). The "pious times" Dryden there longingly recalls, soon replaced by moral, political, and religious corruption, evidently understood and practiced what the Ancients called *pietas*, that is, dutiful conduct toward the gods, one's parents, family, benefactors, and country. Now, as a direct result of the ungodly example of priests, piety, understood as the *pietas* for which Aeneas is the best-known exemplar, is hardly possible. Most important, of course, is the lack of respect for, indeed the insult to, God. It is precisely this sense of piety that Dryden, now committed to ancient ideals, works to restore as he exposes priestcraft as well as the directions of modern thought, accepting the responsibilities he evidently felt the clergy had neglected.

Beginning with *All for Love* in 1677 Dryden consistently and successfully integrated his anticlericalism into theme and structure, emphasizing priestly perfidy and revealing the significance he attached to such clerical failure.[15] If we are to understand the nature, extent, and significance of Dryden's opposition to the clergy in this important period of his life, we must attend to the role churchmen play in his art, a role that has not been sufficiently recognized.

All for Love and its subtitle, *The World Well Lost*, spotlight Dryden's focal concerns in the play. As exemplified in the brilliant imagery, it is in at least one sense about transcendence of the Heraclitean flux and of the depersonalizing and soul-enclosing intrigue that characterizes the "worlds" of both Egypt and Rome. Antony well loses that world in choosing instead the constancy Dryden embodies in Cleopatra's love, "the jewel of great price."[16] More so than is ordinarily realized, *All for Love*'s distinction between transcendent and worldly—if conventional—values, between the private and public, reflects Dryden's own important development: he comes to place his faith not in politics and hopes for scientific and secular progress but rather in the realm of the spirit, which reveals the imprint of God.[17] If this is so, we may readily understand his vituperative treatment of priests, whom he sees as surrogates of Christ in the service of the powers of the world and thus betrayers of the Christ-role they fill.

Though in this play the attention devoted to the clergy is limited, Dryden makes effective use of the priest Serapion. Evidently Serapion has the faults endemic in the priesthood, for Alexas claims that his primary concern is "His offerings" (V.i.). The characterization of Serapion, in the opening scene, as an intriguer foreshadows the play's general theme:

> And dreamed you this? or did invent the story?
> To frighten our Egyptian boys withal,
> And train them up, betimes, in fear of priesthood?
> . . . .
> A foolish dream,
> Bred from the fumes of undigested feasts,
> And holy luxury.

More particularly, Serapion assists in directing the audience's acceptance of Antony and of his rejection of certain orthodoxies. For if following the dictates of one's rational nature is to be approved, conventional obedience to unnatural forms, such as a religion dominated by priests, must appear unworthy. By presenting the representative of religion as corrupt, Dryden helps us accept the unconventional. Further, it is important that Serapion both opens and closes the play. The choice of the priest, rather than the highest ranking surviving character, to take charge at the end may be dramatically unconventional, but it effectively achieves several purposes. It completes the frame and, because Serapion is a symbol of the intrigue and self-interest of the way Antony rejects, Dryden is able to establish the permanence of the world "well lost." Moreover, by framing and in a sense enclosing the tragic pair, Dryden suggests the way they are entrapped in an unfeeling world of self-seeking manipulators. Within the contexts Serapion helps establish, Antony's choice of Cleopatra rather than "the world" appears justified. Dryden's dramatic advocacy of world-transcendence is thus pointedly independent of established religion, which here fosters, rather than retards, the success of the "world."

More striking and more important dramatically is Dryden's

use of the priest in *Troilus and Cressida*. In his version, unlike Chaucer's or Shakespeare's, Cressida is completely faithful to her naive Trojan lóver. Cressida's father, a priest and "a fugitive to the Grecian camp," becomes the instrument or material cause of the eventual tragedy. The truth found too late is that Cressida is not a whore—Calchas is.

In each of several actions leading to the deaths in Act Five Calchas provides the material cause on which various efficient causes work. Prior to the action of the play the priest had fled his homeland and deserted his daughter; though the reason is never made absolutely clear, he had evidently sought revenge for the loss of his priestly office in Troy (IV.ii.).[18] At any rate, as Hector observes, he became "A traitor to his country" (III.ii). Among the Greeks, however, he soon decided that he wanted Cressida with him and managed an exchange for her.[19] Once Cressida is safely by his side, he suddenly expresses his "woman's longing to return" (IV.ii.), further exemplifying the inconstancy that is central to the play's theme. Nowhere regretting or feeling the shame of his desertion of daughter and homeland, he makes Cressida seem important to him only as a means of effecting the desired return to Troy. To manage that, Calchas persuades Cressida that she must "dissemble love" to Diomedes so that, when they are ready to flee the Greek camp, "This Argus then may close his hundred eyes, / And leave our flight more easy" (IV.ii.). Reluctantly Cressida agrees. Troilus knows nothing of this scheme, and so, when he discovers her giving his own ring to Diomedes, he concludes the worst. As the daughter of a priest, Troilus says, she could only be unfaithful: "She sucked the infusion of her father's soul" and therefore "Her soul's a whore already" (IV.ii.). Troilus's behavior in this scene—he spares the life of a prisoner because he too claims to hate priests—helps insure that the audience will consider the priest's role in the tragedy.[20] Later on, with Diomedes and Troilus at each other's throat, Cressida wants to explain her actions to Troilus. "If Troilus die," she tells her father, "I have no share in life." Calchas can think only of his scheme to return to Troy:

If Diomede sink beneath the sword of Troilus,
We lose not only a protector here,
But are debarred all future means of flight.

(V.ii.)

As urged, Cressida intercedes for Diomedes. The result is the Greek's treachery (he falsely claims to have enjoyed full possession of Cressida), and the consequence of that is her suicide.

Why Dryden radically revised the story of Troilus and Cressida, making Calchas rather than his daughter the faithless one, is puzzling. Such a transformation, though, extreme as it is, is in line with Dryden's evident intention at the time to expose clerical treachery whenever and wherever possible. A primary reason for this effort was his growing concern with social unrest and political rebellion and especially a belief that greed and thirst for power made the clergy ready instruments in any cause that promised preferment and "lusty benefices." Whether or not it induced the attention directed to Calchas, Dryden's interest in the worsening political situation appears in *Troilus and Cressida;* by shifting the order of the opening scenes, for example, he, unlike Shakespeare, stresses the civil problems besetting the Greeks and establishes a relevance to England, a point reiterated in the play's last lines: e.g., "since from home-bred factions ruin springs, / Let subjects learn obedience to their kings."

Whenever Dryden focuses on the political situation in the late 1670s and early 1680s, the clergy is treated at some length. In *Absalom and Achitophel,* to take a prominent example, he connects the present upheaval with the "Good old Cause," claims the Dissenting clergy form the vanguard of this movement, and contends that their motivation is the same as that of their predecessors in the 1640s:

With them Joyn'd all th' Haranguers of the Throng,
That thought to get Preferment by the Tongue.

. . . .

Hot *Levites* Headed these; who pul'd before
From th' *Ark,* which in the Judges days they bore,

> Resum'd their Cant, and with a Zealous Cry,
> Pursu'd their old belov'd Theocracy:
> Where Sanhedrin and Priest inslav'd the Nation,
> And justifi'd their Spoils by Inspiration;
> For who so fit for Reign as *Aaron's* Race,
> If once Dominion they could found in Grace?
> These led the Pack; tho not of surest scent,
> Yet deepest mouth'd against the Government.
>   (ll. 509–10, 519–28)

The attack is by no means limited to the "fanatical" clergy, however; as Leon M. Guilhamet notes, Dryden includes even the
Anglican priesthood in the sweeping condemnation.[21] After
charging that "Priests of all Religions are the same" (l. 99), Dryden asserts:

> The *Jewish Rabbins* thô their Enemies,
> In this conclude them honest men and wise:
> For 'twas their duty, all the Learned think,
> T' espouse his Cause by whom they eat and drink.
>   (ll. 104–7)

A few lines later Dryden again directs the charge of materialistic
concern at the Established clergy: the Catholics' "busie Teachers," he says,

> mingled with the *Jews;*
> And rak'd, for Converts, even the Court and Stews:
> Which *Hebrew* Priests the more unkindly took,
> Because the Fleece accompanies the Flock.
>   (ll. 126–29)

The Second Part of *Absalom and Achitophel*, written in collaboration with Nahum Tate and published in 1682, is even more direct
in its denunciation of Anglican churchmen; among those singled out in the parts generally thought to be Dryden's contribu-

tion to the poem are Samuel Johnson, chaplain to the Whig leader William Russell and author of the notorious exclusionist tract *Julian the Apostate* (ll. 350 ff.), and the Latitudinarian Gilbert Burnet (ll. 396–99).[22] In the context of the widespread belief that Catholic priests had long been engaged in the most sinister plots against the king, the government, and the Protestant religion, Dryden's emphasis in both poems on the Dissenting and Anglican clergy, to the virtual exclusion of the Catholic, seems remarkable. The implication seems to be that if Jesuits are unscrupulous, power-hungry, and seditious, they are no different from priests of other religions. Indeed, lines 85–97 appear sympathetic toward the plight of English Catholics.

At any rate, the anticlerical passages are thematically functional in *Absalom and Achitophel*. At the center of the poem and of the current unrest is "the threat of a specific new force in English life: economic, religious, and political individualism." What has happened, as Ronald Paulson puts it, is that a "single ambitious man is willing to overthrow the state in order to gain more power for himself; so he seduces the king's illegitimate son (a pseudo-Christ) into rebelling against his father and master (God), and by means of a plot he turns the crowd into his ally."[23] But the role of the clergy in duping the crowd must not be overlooked. In this regard they are presented as like Shaftesbury and Titus Oates, himself "a *Levite*" (l. 644). Indeed, priests are the corporate manifestation of the evil force represented by Shaftesbury. What Paulson concludes about Shaftesbury applies to the clergy as well: the Satanic focus of the poem "is presented not only as a tempter but as a hypocritical pretender to religion or to public reform: a memory of the fanatic Puritan and the mercenary London merchants who, professing piety, overthrew Charles I."[24] The churchmen satirized in *Absalom and Achitophel* subvert their priestly function as they participate in, and in some cases guide, unholy actions that would, if successful, usher in the reign of man rather than of God.

In *The Duke of Guise*, first performed in 1682, Dryden again depicted the priesthood as agents of sedition and rebellion. He wrote the play in collaboration with Nathaniel Lee, but only those parts he claimed to be his (the first scene, the entire fourth act, and about half of Act Five) expose the central role of the clergy in the Guisard uprising in sixteenth-century France.[25] The play goes far toward justifying the loyalist Crillon's claim that "when the preachers draw against the king, a parson in a pulpit is a devilish fore-horse" (V.i.).

A central figure in the opening scene is the firebrand Curate of Saint Eustace, the most zealous and unprincipled of the Guisards, who says he has "been taking godly pains to satisfy some scruples raised amongst weak brothers of our party, that were staggering in the cause." Bussy and Polin appear bothered by the Curate's methods when he explains how he has eased the troubled consciences of some of their fellow rebels by means of a Calvinist book justifying rebellion against irreligious kings:

> *Buss.* To borrow arguments from heretic books,
> Methinks, was not so prudent.
> *Cur.* Yes; from the devil, if it would help our cause.
> The author was indeed a heretic;
> The matter of the book is good and pious.
> *Pol.* But one prime article of our Holy League
> Is to preserve the king, his power, and person.
> *Cur.* That must be said, you know, for decency;
> A pretty blind to make the shoot secure.
> *Buss.* But did the primitive Christians e'er rebel,
> When under heathen lords? I hope they did.
> *Cur.* No, sure they did not; for they had not power;
> The conscience of a people is their power.

Dryden further illustrates the Curate's sophistic dexterity when he has him proudly proclaim: "I'll make it out: Rebellion is an insurrection against the government; but they that have the power are actually the government; therefore, if the people have the power, the rebellion is in the king." The reasons for the Curate's zeal are plain. According to the Cardinal of Guise, the duke's brother and himself an unscrupulous intriguer,

> . . . he hopes you mean to make him abbot,
> And he deserves your care of his preferment;
> For all his prayers are curses on the government,
> And all his sermons libels on the king;
> In short, a pious, hearty, factious priest.

As the Curate himself puts it, in terms that echo Dryden's charges in *Absalom and Achitophel*: "Heaven's good; the cause is good; the money's good; / No matter whence it comes."

Between this point in the play and the next part Dryden claimed to have written, the clergy have no role. But in the fourth act the priesthood again receives considerable attention. Here, for example, the Cardinal's perfidiousness emerges most clearly. In opposition to the Duke's wishes, he exclaims, referring to the king and echoing the Curate's desire to "despatch him; I love to make all sure" (I.i):

> We have him in our power, cooped in his court.
> Who leads the first attack? Now by yon heaven,
> That blushes at my scarlet robes, I'll doff
> This womanish attire of godly peace,
> And cry,—Lie there, Lord Cardinal of Guise.
> (IV.iii.)

Later on, after the king has forbidden shedding the blood of Crillon and his party, the Cardinal cries:

> What mean you, brother, by this godly talk,
> Of sparing Christian blood? Why, these are dogs;
> Now, by the sword that cut off Malchus' ear,
> Mere dogs, that neither can be saved nor damned.

To insure that we appreciate the pervasiveness of such clerical villainy Dryden shows the Archbishop to be no different from the Curate and the Cardinal. "Where," the Archbishop asks the Duke, "have you learnt to spare inveterate foes?" To the Duke's subsequent objection that "You know the book," the Archbishop replies:

And can expound it too:
But Christian faith was in the nonage then,
And Roman heathens lorded o'er the world.
What madness were it for the weak and few,
To fight against the many and the strong?
Crillon must die, so must the tyrant's guards,
Lest, gathering head again, they make more work.

(IV.iv.)

In the same act, by somewhat different means, Dryden levels other charges against the clergy. In the second scene of Act Four an evil spirit Melanax appears dressed in clerical robe, which prompts the necromancer Malicorne to ask:

But why in this fanatic habit, devil?
Thou look'st like one that preaches to the crowd;
Gospel is in thy face, and outward garb,
And treason on thy tongue.

Melanax responds, making a point regarding scriptural manip-ulation that Dryden himself developed in other places and sug-gesting a connection between the Devil and the priesthood:

Thou hast me right:
Ten thousand devils more are in this habit;
Saintship and zeal are still our best disguise:
We mix unknown with the hot thoughtless crowd,
And quoting Scriptures, (which too well we know,)
With impious glosses ban the holy text,
And make it speak rebellion, schism, and murder;
So turn the arms of heaven against itself.[26]

In the second line here does Melanax refer to actual devils, or is this a metaphor for priests? Similarly, are "Saintship and zeal" disguises for the Devil or priests? Dryden's point seems to be that the two are indistinguishable, and it is even clearer in the fourth scene of Act Four. In the same attire and, according to the stage direction, "at the head of [the citizens]," the Devil Melanax is busy offering the mob "a word of godly exhortation to strengthen your hands, ere you give the onset." When he declares, "To promote sedition is my business," it is not clear whether he is speaking as Devil or priest, which is Dryden's point exactly. "It has been so before any of you were born, and will be so, when you are all dead and damned; I have led on the rabble in all ages." He proudly repeats, "I have sown rebellion everywhere." The Devil and priests alike promote "the cause."

The Spanish Fryar (1681) focuses sharply on clerical corruption. Because the usual interpretation of this play challenges the pattern we have seen developing in Dryden's treatment of the clergy, it deserves considerable attention. I think we will see that this artfully constructed tragicomedy reinforces our understanding of the remarkable degree to which the priesthood was then preying on Dryden's mind as it provides for a better understanding of the exact nature of that concern.

The title would seem to establish the centrality of the unscrupulous friar, but in the most thorough study to date Bruce King claims that Dominic's role is unrelated to the theme, which, he says, points to "a basic incoherence of parts within the play."[27] Commentators by and large have viewed Dominic as an excrescence on what is otherwise agreed to be one of Dryden's most successful plays. Taking their cue from the phrase "a Protestant play" which Dryden wittily employs in the dedication to "a Protestant patron" (John Lord Haughton), scholars have usually seen the depiction of the friar as "an attack upon an obnoxious priesthood whom [Dryden], in common with all the nation, believed to have been engaged in the darkest intrigues against the King and Government."[28] This "crude caricature of Catholicism" thus reflects, says Scott, the poet's participation in "the general ferment which the discovery of the Popish Plot had excited."[29]

In fact, however, the "Popish Plot" did not produce any such

"ferment" in Dryden. In *Absalom and Achitophel* he blames Anglican and Dissenting churchmen for promoting sedition while
extenuating Jesuit blame. Though the clergy depicted in *The
Duke of Guise* necessarily is Catholic, Dryden's primary interest
lies in a general issue of which the situations in sixteenth-century France and seventeenth-century England are particular instances. In *Absalom and Achitophel*, moreover, with admirable
balance Dryden attempts to place the "Plot" in perspective:

> From hence began that Plot, the Nation's Curse,
> Bad in it self, but represented worse:
> Rais'd in extremes, and in extremes decry'd;
> With Oaths affirm'd, with dying Vows deny'd:
> Not weigh'd, or winnow'd by the Multitude;
> But swallow'd in the Mass, unchew'd and Crude.
> Some Truth there was, but dash'd and brew'd with Lyes;
> To please the Fools, and puzzle all the Wise.
> Succeeding times did equal folly call,
> Believing nothing, or believing all.[30]
>
> (ll. 108–17)

Earlier, when almost the entire nation believed Titus Oates's
malicious allegations, Dryden seems to have been no surer of
any such plot. Certainly his casual reference to the "plot" in the
dedication of *The Kind Keeper*, produced when excitement was at
fever pitch, does not suggest the degree of involvement and
even frenzy that Scott claims.

Neither does *The Spanish Fryar*. As Bredvold observes, the
play "is not ornamented . . . with topical allusions to the Popish
Plot and its ramifications."[31] The couple of references to plot-
ting, in fact, seem wittily topical, rather than framed to remind
the audience of grave dangers outside the theatre. If Dryden
were caught up in the "ferment" excited by the "Popish Plot,"
he strangely failed to take advantage of the excellent opportunity *The Spanish Fryar* afforded him to condemn Catholic political intrigue. For the thoroughly corrupt friar is relegated to the

comic plot where his intrigues are pointedly limited to amorous rather than political causes. The Catholic priesthood here as elsewhere is the obvious vehicle of Dryden's assault on the clergy, rather than the sole or perhaps even the primary object of a partisan attack. As in Dryden's other major treatments of churchmen (*The Indian Emperour, Troilus and Cressida, The Duke of Guise, Don Sebastian,* and "The Character of a Good Parson"), the priesthood satirized is not limited to the clergy directly presented. Dryden's strategy and purpose in *The Spanish Fryar* have not been correctly perceived.[32]

Without attempting a full-scale vindication of Dryden's own view, supported by Dr. Johnson, that the serious and comic plots fit well together, I think we can appreciate Dominic's relation, indeed centrality, to the whole. As King has noted, *The Spanish Fryar* is designed in part to show that "rebellion, for any reason, is against the will of God."[33] But in addition to answering the central political and theological questions raised by demonstrating that, contrary to earlier appearances, a providential power exists that, according to the play's conclusion, "guards the sacred lives of kings" and involves itself in the daily affairs of men, the play also dramatizes the human tendencies that often conflict with the moral order built into the nature of things. Leonora's soliloquy in III.iii. poses exactly the question of the relationship of men's actions to the Divine Will. Leonora admits the evil with which human activity is tainted, though she denies responsibility for her own actions, maintaining that they have been determined by Heaven; her own consent to Sancho's death, she rationalizes, is proof of Heaven's concurrence:

> . . . I would not do this crime,
> And yet, like heaven, permit it to be done.
> The priesthood grossly cheat us with free-will:
> Will to do what—but what heaven first decreed?
> Our actions then are neither good nor ill,
> Since from eternal causes they proceed;
> Our passions,—fear and anger, love and hate,—

> Mere senseless engines that are moved by fate;
> Like ships on stormy seas, without a guide,
> Tossed by the winds, and driven by the tide.

I would contend that, rather than merely an argument against political rebellion, *The Spanish Fryar* is in large part about these passions in relation to the existing moral order. The play suggests the necessity of restraining, rather than indulging, the self-seeking and impetuous will.

Alike in fundamental ways, both plots concentrate on the failure to curb human willfulness. This failure, which occurs in all the major characters except Torrismond, takes several forms. On the private level it appears in the predatory "courtship" of the cynical libertine Lorenzo and the lusty Elvira, who readily accepts the advice to dispatch her old, jealous, and avaricious husband Gomez. It is also present in Bertran's similarly vicious counsel to the Queen regarding a parallel situation; he advises her to "Remove this threatening danger from your Crown [the old king], / And then securely take the man you love" (III.iii.). Raymond's abortive rebellion against Leonora and Torrismond simply extends into the public sector this theme of the willfulness of fallen human nature. A proud attempt "to effect divine justice, instead of depending upon the ways of providence,"[34] this political episode is but one of several similar situations embodying the play's theme, rather than the vehicle which carries the burden of Dryden's meaning.

Despite the competition, the corrupt friar emerges as the most selfish, incontinent character in *The Spanish Fryar*. Dominic's very appearance symbolizes what he is. The first description of him, coming early in the opening scene as an example of the frenzied fear besetting the city, reveals his self-indulgence:

> I met a reverend, fat, old gouty friar,—
> With a paunch swoln so high, his double chin
> Might rest upon it; a true son of the Church;
> Fresh-coloured, and well-thriven on his trade,—

Come puffing with his greasy bald-pate choir,
And fumbling o'er his beads in such an agony,
He told them false, for fear. About his neck
There hung a wench, the label of his function,
Whom he shook off, i'faith, methought, unkindly,
It seems the holy stallion durst not score
Another sin before he left the world.

Even Lorenzo is shocked by Dominic, especially after his only slightly veiled advice to murder the troublesome Gomez, whose jewels they seek and whose wife the friar works to give to the libertine: "The wickedness of this old villain startles me, and gives me a twinge for my own sin, though it was far short of his" (IV.i.). It would be tedious—as well as unnecessary—to document the friar's greed, gluttony, lechery, hypocrisy, pride, and willful practice of other sins. Suffice it to say that Lorenzo is correct in asserting that self-interest determines all his actions: "He preaches against sin; why? because he gets by it: He holds his tongue; why? because so much more is bidden for his silence" (III.ii.). As Lorenzo discovers, having been taught a lesson in selfishness, "There's no trusting this friar's conscience; he has renounced me already more heartily than e'er he did the devil, and is in a fair way to prosecute me for putting on these holy robes. This is the old church-trick; the clergy is ever at the bottom of the plot, but they are wise enough to slip their own necks out of the collar, and leave the laity to be fairly hanged for it" (III.ii.).

Dominic, of course, is not only willfully self-indulgent, but he also panders to the lower appetites of others, provided enough is paid for his services. After the friar's efforts have smoothed the way for Lorenzo and Elvira to satisfy their lust, a relationship that if consummated would have been incestuous, the young woman observes, "This friar is a comfortable man! He will understand nothing of the business, and yet does it all" (II.iii.). As her advice at the end of this scene makes clear, the friar virtually parodies the clerical function: "Pray, wives and

virgins, at your time of need, / For a true guide, of my good father's breed." Of no small consolation to frail nature, moreover,
is his readiness to absolve offenders of sins committed with his
help. As Elvira gratefully acknowledges, "Of what am I afraid,
then? Not my conscience, that's safe enough; my ghostly father
has given it a dose of church-opium, to lull it. Well, for soothing
sin, I'll say that for him, he's a chaplain for any court in Christendom" (III.ii.). Dominic's complete perversion of his function
is neatly summarized in her concluding remark: "we are both
beholding to Friar Dominic; the church is an indulgent mother,
she never fails to do her part" (V.ii.).

In specifically defining the Christian religion in terms of its
opposition to self-interest and indulgence of the natural appetites, *Religio Laici,* written within a year or two of this play,
provides an excellent gloss on the friar:

> This *onely* Doctrine does our *Lusts* oppose:
> Unfed by Natures Soil, in which it grows;
> Cross to our *Interests,* curbing Sense, and Sin;
> Oppress'd without, and undermin'd within,
> It thrives through pain; its own Tormentours tires;
> And with a stubborn patience still aspires.
>
> (ll. 158–63)

Understandably Dryden excludes Dominic from the symbolic
restoration of community at play's end. Though so many others
bearing guilt are excused, the friar alone is punished because he
represents the antithesis of the play's value system, of priestly
comportment, and indeed of the Christian religion. Appropriately he has been compared to the serpent in the Garden (V.ii.)
and to Judas (II.iii.). Gomez for once speaks for Dryden when
he says to Dominic, "Such churchmen as you would make any
man an infidel" (IV.i.).

It seems plain that *The Spanish Fryar* carries a generalized
attack on the clergy, rather than a militant anti-Catholicism
excited by recent events and rumors. The numerous abusive
statements made about the clergy by various characters certainly

extends the ridicule to the clergy generally, though some of the abuse admittedly is directed at friars in particular. The most important of these generalized comments appear in III.ii. in a heated exchange involving Lorenzo, Gomez, and the friar. It begins when Lorenzo charges, in terms that "would not have been lost on the audience at the Duke's Theatre in 1680,"[35] that "the clergy is ever at the bottom of the plot, but they are wise enough to slip their own necks out of the collar, and leave the laity to be fairly hanged for it." Gomez then interjects, "Put pride, hypocrisy, and gluttony into your scale, father, and you shall weigh against me: Nay, an' sins come to be divided once, the clergy puts in for nine parts, and scarce leaves the laity a tithe." "How dar'st thou reproach the tribe of Levi?" Dominic cries. Gomez's response recalls the hostility characteristic of the layman's faiths and at least implicit in so many of Dryden's own works: "Marry, because you make us laymen of the tribe of Issachar. You make asses of us, to bear your burthens. When we are young, you put panniers upon us with your church-discipline; and when we are grown up, you load us with a wife: after that you procure for other men, and then you load our wives too."

An excellent gloss on the play's strategy is provided by the Epilogue, which extends the attack on the clergy and where the opening focus on the Catholic priesthood soon broadens to take in all churchmen. Whether or not Dryden himself wrote the lines is immaterial for our purposes.

> How are men cozened still with shows of good!
> The bawd's best mask is the grave friar's hood;
> Though vice no more a clergyman displeases,
> Than doctors can be thought to hate diseases.
> 'Tis by your living ill, that they live well,
> By your debauches, their fat paunches swell.
> 'Tis a mock war between the priest and devil;
> When they think fit, they can be very civil.
> As some, who did French counsels most advance,
> To blind the world, have railed in print at France,
> Thus do the clergy at your vices bawl,

> That with more ease they may engross them all.
> By damning yours, they do their own maintain;
> A churchman's godliness is always gain:
> Hence to their prince they will superior be;
> And civil treason grows church loyalty.
> They boast the gift of heaven is in their power;—
> Well may they give the god, they can devour!
> Still to the sick and dead their claims they lay;
> For 'tis on carrion that the vermin prey.[36]

The end result in both Epilogue and play is a demeaning and diminishing of the clergy.

The final and most devastating blow to the priesthood comes at the end of the play with the necessary intervention of Providence to undo the friar's roguery: "How vainly man designs, when heaven opposes" (IV.ii.). In one of the double discoveries alluded to in the subtitle, Providence, working through secondary means, thwarts the unwitting and licentious lovers and saves them from incest, just as it brings about in the political sphere what rash men like Raymond, depending on their own power, endanger. Indeed, the final discovery (regarding Sancho) appears in the last few lines of the play, which thus blatantly exploits the *deus ex machina* in order to stress providential intervention. Providence works, moreover, not to punish those who rail at the church, as Dominic would have his many antagonists believe,[37] but rather to punish the churchman who violates and undermines the laws of Heaven. The play thus shows that Providence must sometimes work without and even despite priests, whose responsibility it is to make clear and assist the Will of God. Pedro's comment in the opening scene, "O religion and roguery, how they go together!," both anticipates the first line of *Absalom and Achitophel* and foreshadows an important dramatized point of the play. *The Spanish Fryar*, I suggest, is "a Protestant play" not because it abuses the Catholic religion but because, in the antisacerdotal spirit fundamental to Protestantism, it minimizes the priesthood.

In its emphasis on fallen man's willful inclinations, *The Spanish Fryar* points to the major themes of the works Dryden wrote
during the years immediately following the "Popish Plot." Suggested in this play and explored from the political and theological perspectives in *Absalom and Achitophel* and *Religio Laici*, the
issue at bottom is the fateful question, in whom does final authority and power reside, man or God?

Having finally recognized that Dryden was no hireling who
merely wrote on demand for the party in power, many of us are
now likely to agree that characteristically Dryden's real subject
in his most famous political poem is "a *tertium quid*, an abstract,
general statement of which the English and biblical situations
are merely particular instances."[38] Indeed, there is a growing—
and quite proper—understanding that Dryden wrote less for
Charles than for a transcendent order imaged, though imper-
fectly, by his reign. Dryden's work in this period is often political, at least in appearance, because politics was the arena in
which the fundamental human drama was then being played
out. Paradoxically, Dryden's most political work, superficially
speaking, came about when he had lost faith in the world as the
realm wherein man might achieve some form of redemption and
salvation. At any rate, in the final analysis his argument is that
the current "rebellion" against the king, reflected in the agita-
tion to exclude his Catholic brother from the throne, manifests
opposition to God. According to *The Medall* (1682):

> If Sovereign Right by Sovereign Pow'r they scan,
> The same bold Maxime holds in God and Man:
> God were not safe, his Thunder cou'd they shun
> He shou'd be forc'd to crown another Son.
> (ll. 214–17)

Dryden is not, I think, simply rehearsing the traditional *jure di-
vino* contention that rebellion against the monarch as God's
vicegerent on earth, divinely appointed for that purpose, serving by his express wish, and enjoying his special protection, vio-

lates God's Will. More than this, he finds forces at work which seem to threaten destruction of obligation to and reliance on external authority generally; these forces appear bent on toppling God himself in order to enthrone self-sufficient man. The aim of the new reformers, Dryden claims in *Absalom and Achitophel*, is nothing less than "At once Divine and Humane Laws [to] controul" and so "To change Foundations, cast the Frame anew" (ll. 807, 805). In like manner he wrote in *His Majesties Declaration Defended*, also in 1681, that the king's enemies "will lose their time no more, in cutting off the Succession, altering the course of Nature, and directing the providence of God."[39]

Appropriately, therefore, Dryden associates the current reformers with Satan, the archetypal rebel against God's established order. Thus in *The Spanish Fryar* when Raymond sophistically asks, "What treason is it to redeem my king, / And to reform the state" (his real aim, he has admitted, is to "ruin" the queen and her lover), the heroic Torrismond replies: "That's a stale cheat; / The primitive rebel, Lucifer, first used it, / And was the first reformer of the skies" (V.ii.). The Miltonic echoes throughout *Absalom and Achitophel* help to establish "the false *Achitophel*," "A Name to all succeeding Ages Curst" (ll. 150–51), as "the intrepid Devil himself emerging from Hell to destroy Eden and to devote man to death."[40] The poem's central passage is replete with images of the Garden as Achitophel employs Satan's arguments both there and in the desert, infusing in Absalom-Adam-Christ the deadly poison and precipitating as the event of the temptation another fall. Attempting "with studied Arts to please," Achitophel "sheds his Venome" (ll. 228–29) as follows:

> Auspicious Prince! at whose Nativity
> Some Royal Planet rul'd the Southern sky;
> Thy longing Countries Darling and Desire;
> Their cloudy Pillar, and their guardian Fire:
> Their second *Moses*, whose extended Wand
> Divides the Seas, and shews the promis'd Land:
> Whose dawning Day, in every distant age,

Has exercis'd the Sacred Prophets rage:
The Peoples Prayer, the glad Deviners Theam,
The Young-mens Vision, and the Old mens Dream!
Thee, *Saviour*, Thee, the Nations Vows confess;
And, never satisfi'd with seeing, bless:

. . . .

Believe me, Royal Youth, thy Fruit must be,
Or gather'd Ripe, or rot upon the Tree.
Heav'n, has to all allotted, soon or late,
Some lucky Revolution of their Fate:
Whose Motions, if we watch and guide with Skill,
(For humane Good depends on humane Will,)
Our Fortune rolls, as from a smooth Descent,
And, from the first Impression, takes the Bent:
But, if unseiz'd, she glides away like wind;
And leaves repenting Folly far behind.

(ll. 230–41, 250–59)

If Absalom becomes savior—Dryden's later use of this terminology in ironically describing the "Progress" of the "young *Messiah*" through "the promis'd Land" (ll. 723 ff.) diminishes the possibility that the rhetoric is merely fanciful—politics has evidently replaced religion as the instrument of man's redemption and salvation.[41]

To effect the subversion of order Achitophel has in mind, other hands are needed. Thus he who "Disdain'd the Golden fruit to gather free, / [Also] lent the Croud his Arm to shake the Tree" (ll. 202–3). In fact, it is the argument of the later, darker, and more bitter *Medall* that Shaftesbury, there diminished in stature but still Satanic, has "pox'd" the nation (l. 266). Like Friar Dominic, Flecknoe, and Shadwell a false legislator, he is

. . . the Pander of the Peoples hearts,
(O Crooked Soul, and Serpentine in Arts,)
Whose blandishments a Loyal Land have whor'd,
And broke the Bonds she plighted to her Lord.

(ll. 256–59)

Having seduced "the Croud" as he "ruined" Absalom, Shaftes-bury encourages self-sufficient individualism and its ultimate social consequence, political chaos:

> . . . this new *Jehu* spurs the hot mouth'd horse;
> Instructs the Beast to know his native force;
> To take the Bit between his teeth and fly
> To the next headlong Steep of Anarchy.
>
> (ll. 119–22)

But Dryden makes clear that the consequences are not simply social and political. Now infused with his poison and set "in the Papal Chair" (l. 87), the people reflect Achitophel–Satan's false image: "So all are God-a'mighties" (l. 110).[42]

The clergy's role in this grand enterprise of uncreation must not be forgotten. In light of the foregoing, Dryden's identifica-tion of the priesthood with the Devil in *The Duke of Guise* appears to be of substance. The same suggestion of priestly complicity in the subversion of order results from the links *Ab-salom and Achitophel* establishes between the arch-tempter and the clergy. The "Hot *Levites*," important in crying up "Religion, and Redress of Grievances, / Two names, that always cheat and always please" (ll. 747–48), pursue "their old belov'd Theocra-cy" (l. 522); leading "the Pack," they are "deepest mouth'd against the Government" (ll. 527–28). Of the "numerous Host of dreaming Saints" who follow these priests Dryden says, "'Gainst Form and Order they their Power employ; / Nothing to Build and all things to Destroy" (ll. 529, 531–32), invoking the Satanic determination expressed in Beelzebub's famous declara-tion "either with Hell fire / To waste his whole Creation, or pos-sess / All as our own."[43]

A major weapon of those who plead the cause of "Religion" is Scripture. In the Preface to *Religio Laici* Dryden charges that "those Texts of Scripture, which are not necessary to Salvation, [have been 'detorted'] to the damnable uses of Sedition, distur-bance and destruction of the Civil Government." As he demonstrates in *The Duke of Guise,* Scripture is particularly dangerous in the hands of unscrupulous clergymen, who

> With impious glosses ban the holy text,
> And make it speak rebellion, schism, and murder;
> So turn the arms of heaven against itself.
>
> (IV.ii.)

"False *Achitophel*" also perverts scriptural meaning. In work after work during the early 1680s Dryden focuses on such manipulation of Holy Scripture, which becomes a central element in his "pious" concern with the proper relationship of man to God. This concern is a crucial but largely neglected context for *Religio Laici.*[44]

Abuse of Scripture is nothing new, Dryden maintains. The holy text has perhaps always been a ready weapon for any self-seeking party to use. In the Preface to *Religio Laici,* the structural center of which poem is the "digression" on the new English translation of Father Simon's *Critical History of the Old Testament,* Dryden declares that "While we were Papists, our Holy Father rid us, by pretending authority out of the Scriptures to depose Princes; when we shook off his Authority, the Sectaries furnish'd themselves with the same Weapons; and out of the same Magazine, the Bible." Scripture itself, he admits, is partly to blame; because of its ambiguity on certain nonessential points of faith, it can easily be made to say whatever one pleases. As he put it in the Dedication of *Plutarch's Lives,* "the same Reasons, and Scriptures, which are urg'd by Popes for the deposition of Princes, are produc'd by Sectaries for altering the Succession."[45] Dryden's concern at this time, however, is not with Catholic manipulation of Scripture but with the "Sedition, disturbance and destruction of the Civil Government" threatened by the Whiggish and Dissenting reformers who effectively wield Scripture. The origin of this particular abuse Dryden traces to the Reformation, claiming in the Preface to his layman's faith, "Since the Bible has been Translated into our Tongue, ['the Fanaticks, or Schismaticks, of the *English* Church'] have us'd it so, as if their business was not to be sav'd but to be damnd by its Contents." He goes on in the Preface to charge that "never since the Reformation, has there wanted a Text of [the Fanaticks'] interpreting to authorize a Rebel."[46] His conclusion is not heartening to a Protestant: "If we consider onely them, better had it been for the *English* Nation, that it had still remain'd in the original *Greek* and *Hebrew*, or at least in the honest *Latine* of St. *Jerome*, than that several Texts in it, should have been prevaricated to the destruction of that Government, which put it into so ungrateful hands."

Though he repeatedly abjures the sectarians' convenient habit of neglecting the plain sense of Scripture in favor of undue emphasis on those obscure passages which should be left alone because unnecessary to salvation, Dryden's primary quarrel seems to be with the premise from which such effects follow. That is the fundamental Protestant insistence not only on the availability of Scripture in English translation for every person learned or ignorant but also on Bible reading accompanied by the doctrine of private interpretation. Without at all wishing to imply that Dryden was crypto-Catholic by the early 1680s, I submit that his objection is essentially that of Catholicism to Protestantism. In the Postscript to his translation of Maimbourg's *History of the League* (1684), for example, Dryden speaks contemptuously of the "gift of interpreting Scriptures by private Persons, without Learning" and proceeds to argue that this "was certainly the Original Cause of such Cabals in the Reform'd Churches: So dangerous an instrument of Rebellion is the Holy Scripture, in the hands of ignorant and bigoted men."[47] As he echoes numerous Catholic apologists, Dryden thus opposes the Protestant position as expressed in this representative statement by John Tillotson in his sermon "The Necessity of the Knowledge of the Holy Scriptures": "though there be many difficulties and obscurities in the Scriptures, enough to exercise the skill and wit of the learned, yet are they not therefore either useless or dangerous to the People."[48] Compare this with John Vincent Canes's Catholic position in *Fiat Lux:* "Experience hath now taught us clear enough, that the Scripture is a dangerous edged tool to put into the hands of the rude and boisterous vulgar. . . . [T]he whole and very text now in this last age put into vulgar hands . . . hath filled the land with so much wretchlesness and divisions."[49] Dryden's reiterated point is similar. Perhaps more pessimistic than a year or so earlier, Dryden in 1684 concludes that as long as private interpretation is allowed, Scripture will be manipulated and distorted for selfish ends: "the Scriptures interpreted by each to their own purpose, is always the best weapon in the strongest hand: Observe them all along, and Providence is still the prevailing Argument: They who happen to be in power, will ever urge it against those who are undermost; as they who are depress'd, will never fail to call it Persecution."[50]

Individual interpretation of Scripture is especially dangerous, according to Dryden, when the means is the private spirit. In the Postscript to the *History of the League* he asserts:

["Gods people" have] had the impudence to pretend to Inspiration in the Exposition of Scriptures; a trick which since [the Reformation] has been familiarly us'd by every Sect, in its turn, to advance their interests. Not content with this, they assum'd to themselves a more particular intimacy with Gods Holy Spirit; as if it guided them, even beyond the power of the Scriptures, to know more of him than was therein taught: For now the Bible began to be a dead Letter, of it self; and no virtue was attributed to the reading of it, but all to the inward man, the call of the Holy Ghost, and the ingrafting of the Word, opening their Understanding to hidden Mysteries by Faith: And here the Mountebank way of canting words came first in use: as if there were something more in Religion than cou'd be express'd in intelligible terms, or Nonsense were the way to Heaven. This of necessity must breed divisions amongst them; for every mans Inspiration being particular to himself, must clash with anothers, who set up for the same qualification.[51]

This important passage summarizes Dryden's concern in the early 1680s with approaches to Scripture, makes clear the atomistic individualism and proliferation of sects that he sees resulting from private interpretation, and suggests that a man's way of treating Scripture reflects his relationship to God, whose Revealed Word the Bible is. The sectarians' approach to Scripture, by means of which God's Word becomes "a dead Letter, of it self" and thus subordinate to the intervening private spirit, emerges as symptomatic of the general tendency Dryden has been concerned with to remove God and install an unholy substitute of man's own devising.

Exactly this point Dryden vigorously asserted two years earlier in *The Medall*, where he contends that Scripture will almost certainly be victimized because helpless before willful interpreters. After observing that the Protestant sects "rack ev'n Scripture" and "plead a Call to preach, in spight of Laws" (ll. 156–57), he writes:

> But that's no news to the poor injur'd Page;
> It has been us'd as ill in every Age:
> And is constrain'd, with patience, all to take;
> For what defence can *Greek* and *Hebrew* make?
> Happy who can this talking Trumpet seize;
> They make it speak whatever Sense they please!
> 'Twas fram'd, at first, our Oracle t' enquire;
> But, since our Sects in prophecy grow higher,
> The Text inspires not them; but they the Text inspire.
>
> (ll. 158–66)

Displacing God in obliterating his Word, these private interpreters turn Scripture into an image of themselves, a counterfeit. Impetuous and tyrannized by the self, the sectarians create a meaning that reflects themselves, rather than seeking to find the meaning visible to those who take no private road. Their obtrusion upon God's Word bodies forth their usurpation of his authority and place and thus participates in the work of uncreation carried on by the reformers who set out "To change Foundations, cast the Frame anew" as well as by false prophets like Flecknoe and Shadwell, whose "art" denies access to Nature, imaging only its antithesis. Believing in the failure of both poet and priest at once to expose the Satanic inversions and to keep open access to Being, Dryden lashes both groups in works that point to the eternal struggle imaged in the current religiopolitical conflict. Dryden's most complex, and least appreciated, contribution to this effort was *Religio Laici*, where, through a focus on Scripture as God's Revealed Word, he seeks to reestablish a proper, that is, pious, relationship to God and thereby to all authority outside the self.

4

The Unresolved Conflict
of Dryden's Layman's Faith

Dryden claimed that reading Henry Dickinson's translation of
The Critical History of the Old Testament "bred" his *Religio Laici*
(l. 226).[1] Evidently what he meant was that Father Simon's con-
troversial and epochal work not only provided an opportunity
to focus on issues of continuing importance to him but also suggested a way to construct a poem that would address the current
religiopolitical situation as it explored the implications of various
approaches to scriptural meaning. The result, in any case, is a
public poem with a specific argument that yet contains Dryden's
own individual expression of faith. The nature of the particular
argument presented reflects—because derived from—Dryden's
own understanding at that moment; the poem cannot, therefore, be divorced from the poet's biography.

I begin with the question of genre, perhaps "the most important question an interpreter could ask about a text, since its answer implies the way the text should be understood with respect
to its shape and emphasis as well as the scope and direction of
its meanings."[2] Now we have already determined that *Religio
Laici* fulfills its title and subtitle, but this tells us practically nothing about its literary status nor, more specifically, the literary
genre to which it belongs. I shall argue that the poem requires
that we bring a quite different set of expectations to bear on it
from those of critics who believe *Religio Laici* to be a proselike

tract arranging borrowed and conventional arguments in a purely logical progression and distinguished from numerous prose
apologetics only by a superimposed "poetic dress" that has no
effect on meaning; reading the poem as if it were ordinary prose
results in the equation of its meaning with the apologetical
sources Dryden has employed.

In the Preface Dryden makes clear the literary kind to which
Religio Laici belongs:

> The Verses were written for an ingenious young Gentle-
> man my Friend; upon his Translation of *The Critical History
> of the Old Testament*, compos'd by the learned Father *Simon*:
> The Verses therefore are address'd to the Translatour of
> that Work, and the style of them is, what it ought to be,
> Epistolary.
>
> If any one be so lamentable a Critique as to require the
> Smoothness, the Numbers and the Turn of Heroick Poetry
> in this Poem; I must tell him, that if he has not read *Horace*,
> I have studied him, and hope the style of his Epistles is not
> ill imitated here.

The style of the Horatian epistles would seem well suited to a
layman's faith, which would be enriched by the precedential invocation of the poet highly regarded as a moral instructor and
indeed often "Christianized." At any rate, Dryden's choice of
genre determines not only his style but also the tone, structure,
and movement of the poem, as well as the employment of inter-
locutors or *adversarii*.[3]

As Eduard Fraenkel observes, "Philosophical problems had
been discussed in letters before, and letters in verse had occa-
sionally been written before, but nothing comparable to Horace's *Epistles* had ever existed in Greek or Roman literature";[4]
they are serious discourses written in the style of the *sermones*.
Affecting what Pope called "graceful Negligence," Horace sought
to capture in his twenty *Epistles* the qualities of actual conversation. "More properly Talking upon Paper, than Writing,"[5] these
"letters" exhibit abrupt transitions, frequent modulation of tone

and change in tempo, in short, the appearance of spontaneity. Horace himself speaks in the "letters" as a witty and urbane companion, amiable and well bred, balancing the personal and impersonal and maintaining the *aequus animus* even when he attacks. Though he does not parade his seriousness, just as he conceals his artistry, Horace is, in Dryden's terms, "perpetually moral"; as one early eighteenth-century writer put it, Horace "shews the *Gentleman* even whilst he reads the most serious Lectures of *Philosophy*."[6] Reuben A. Brower finely summarizes the characteristics of the *Epistles*: they exhibit, he says, "the freewheeling of the ideal conversationalist who now speaks to his listener as friend-to-friend, who next talks to himself as he speculates or expresses some personal desire, who at times stands aside to let a piece of comic dialogue or narrative speak for itself, who can without embarrassment take the part of an orator or a lyric poet or philosopher."[7] Though perhaps not as strictly as Pope in the *Imitations*, Dryden follows the Horatian mode in his layman's faith.

Certainly the style of *Religio Laici*, sometimes cited as the purest illustration of "poetry of statement," exhibits the plainness characteristic of the *Epistles*. Dryden in fact used the same terms to describe his poem and the Latin prototype, modestly stating in *Religio Laici* that "this unpolish'd, rugged Verse, I chose; / As fittest for Discourse, and nearest Prose" (ll. 453–54) and later terming the *Epistles* "*sermoni propiora*, nearer prose than verse."[8] But, disconcertingly to many readers, Dryden's poem is not uniformly "prosey." The poem, in fact, reveals a broad range of styles, framing the predominantly plain style. The final couplet of the overwhelmingly plain concluding verse paragraph is low and decidedly "unpoetic": "For, while from *Sacred Truth* I do not swerve, / *Tom Sternhold*'s, or *Tom Sha———ll*'s *Rhimes* will serve." In vivid contrast is the exordium, strikingly figurative and justly celebrated for its rich imagery, the most characteristic device of poetry.[9]

The variation in style results in large part from the frequent changes in tone. Dryden modulates along a broad spectrum of tones, ranging from the serious, even magisterial opening to the playful, facetious, and flippant ending, and from the exaggerated praise of Henry Dickinson at the geographical center of the poem to the contemptuous and crude treatment of the "Fanaticks." The local effects achieved may be illustrated with reference to the *"Systeme of Deisme"* and Dryden's response thereto. He presents the Deist's creed in plain language; the Deist speaks straightforwardly, almost reportorially: *"God* is that *Spring* of *Good; Supreme,* and *Best; / We,* made to *serve,* and in that Service *blest"* (ll. 44–45). Dryden's response, however, is personal and emotional, mingling pity and scorn: "Vain, wretched Creature, how art thou misled / To think thy Wit these God-like Notions bred!" (ll. 64–65). Then, at lines 93–98, raising the pitch, he begins to lash out, satirically:

> Dar'st thou, poor Worm, offend *Infinity?*
> And must the Terms of Peace be given by *Thee?*
> Then *Thou* art *Justice* in the *last Appeal;*
> *Thy easie God* instructs Thee to *rebell:*
> And, like a King remote, and weak, must take
> What Satisfaction *Thou* art pleas'd to make.

Immediately the tone changes again; the biting edge gone, Dryden proceeds on a different level to deflate his opponent's argument:

> But if there be a *Pow'r* too *Just* and *strong*
> To wink at *Crimes,* and bear unpunish'd *Wrong;*
> Look humbly upward, see his Will disclose
> The *Forfeit* first, and then the *Fine* impose.
>   (ll. 99–102)

Similar diversity of tone, often satirical, appears in the verse paragraphs dealing, respectively, with Catholic and sectarian abuse of Scripture (ll. 370–426).

Dryden's skillful use of Deist and Catholic speakers to represent and embody positions he opposes helps enliven and give further variety to what thus appears as an extended conversation involving people rather than abstractions; Dryden's use of the rhetorical device of *adversarius* derives, of course, from Horace. The conversational tone is supported by direct address, not only to the adversaries but also to Dickinson, the ostensible recipient of the "letter": e.g., "'Tis true, my Friend, (and far be Flattery hence)" (l. 398). Moreover, Dryden achieves a Horatian air of spontaneity through elements of the poem's structure, which often reflects not the logical arrangement of ideas but rather the informality and natural flow of talk. Certain passages, like the vituperative address to the Deist at lines 93–98, cannot be explained in terms of logical necessity. Rather, these lines represent the movement of the speaker's mind and reflect the increasing heat of his opposition to a *"Systeme"*—that notion is itself repugnant to the gentlemanly speaker—that he finds religiously and politically dangerous.

The Horatian quality of the poem, with its expected emphasis on the nature of the speaking voice, is perhaps most apparent in the so-called digression on the translator of the *Critical History*. These self-reflexive lines seem to interrupt the ongoing argument, only to channel the thought in a new direction. Certainly Dryden's address to his young friend, delivered in a casual and sometimes bantering tone, captures the spirit of Horace's *Epistles*, including their characteristic freedom of surface movement. This section opens on the rhetorically effective claim that the speaker was guided in the preceding argument by the greatest of the Christian virtues and proceeds to show him as humble and even self-deprecating as he again calls attention to the amateurish nature of his efforts, arriving at last at the praise of Father Simon's translator, which, coming from an urbane man addressing a friend, is playfully complex and witty.[10]

> Thus far my Charity this path has try'd;
> (A much unskilfull, but well meaning guide:)
> Yet what they are, ev'n these crude thoughts were bred
> By reading that, which better thou hast read:
> Thy Matchless Author's work: which thou, my Friend,
> By well translating better dost commend:

Those youthfull hours which, of thy Equals most
In *Toys* have *squander'd*, or in *Vice* have *lost*,
Those hours hast thou to Nobler use employ'd;
And the severe Delights of Truth enjoy'd.

(ll. 224–33)

When Dryden turns from praising Dickinson to the work he has recently translated, the badinage becomes less playful and somewhat more serious. Emerging fully is the voice of the urbane layman, no friend of "crabbed Toil," generally skeptical of the narrowly professional, who makes sport of Father Simon's "weighty" efforts. Perhaps anticipating Swift's and Pope's rejection of scientism, the speaker finds it difficult to take with complete seriousness the priest's scholarly endeavor, an example of the rigorous textual criticism Pope would condemn in another learned man as blatant duncery. To the layman the *Critical History*, a prolegomenon to a new and accurate translation of the Old Testament, appeared weighty "in every sense, ponderous as well as heavy, deep but also dull." [11]

Witness this weighty Book, in which appears
The crabbed Toil of many thoughtfull years,
Spent by thy Authour, in the Sifting Care
Of *Rabbins* old Sophisticated Ware
From Gold Divine; which he who well can sort
May afterwards make *Algebra* a Sport:
A Treasure, which if *Country-Curates* buy,
They *Junius*, and *Tremellius* may defy:
Save pains in various readings, and Translations;
And without *Hebrew* make most learn'd quotations.

(ll. 234–43)

The wit here is at the expense not only of the country clergy but also of the scholarly French Jesuit. Without specifically condemning or even directly criticizing the priest's work, the last few verses place his long and arduous labor in a quite unacademically realistic context, where the painstaking scholarship is

interpreted as a crutch for lonely, perhaps ignorant, and lazy cu-
rates, rather than seen, as the priest intended, as a notable contribution to the search for truth. Then having blunted the effect
of the *Critical History*, thought by Bossuet and Evelyn to aim
"deadly blowes" at the very roots of Christianity itself,[12] Dryden
abandons the bantering tone and proceeds to genuine praise.
The book, he says, is

> A Work so full with various Learning fraught,
> So nicely pondred, yet so strongly wrought,
> As Natures height and Arts last hand requir'd:
> As much as Man cou'd compass, uninspir'd.
>   (ll. 244–47)

He goes on to claim that the real significance of the *Critical History* lies in its apparently unintentional but accurate testimony to
the ways in which certain "Interests" appear prominently in the
transmission of Scripture, interests that are later identified with
the church and as here are construed as incriminating Catholicism (l. 275). Thanks to the priest's unclericallike effort (Dryden
praises him as "not too *much* a *Priest*," l. 253),

> . . . we may see what *Errours* have been made
> Both in the *Copiers* and *Translaters Trade*:
> How *Jewish*, *Popish*, Interests have prevail'd,
> And where *Infallibility* has *fail'd*.
>   (ll. 248–51)

Analysis of the "Digression" establishes Dryden's character
as projected in the poem.[13] Wary of self-assertiveness; generally
tentative; undogmatic; amiable in the emphatic charitableness
that permeates both poem and Preface; urbane in his wide-rang-
ing knowledge and familiarity with traditional wisdom; pol-
ished, easy, and graceful as he addresses friend and opponents,
discusses "Sacred things," and moves among subtle and conflicting arguments, the Dryden we see in *Religio Laici* recalls
Horace and implies the civilization that he had come to repre-

sent for the late seventeenth century. Given this character, which figures most prominently in the conversations with the Deist and the Catholics (there are two Catholic speakers), it is not surprising that the alternative proposed to the dangerous positions of the three major opponents is moderate, described in moral and theological terms, and reminiscent of the Horatian *via media*.

A layman's faith expressed as a Horatian epistle, *Religio Laici* is first of all a poem. Because it is, we must attend closely to resonances which not only enrich but create meaning. Ultimately, we must seek out the center of the poetic movement, which unfolds the poem's inner laws and its aim.[14]

It is a mistake to view the poem literally and as a purely logical development of the ideas taken from apologetical sources. An outline of the first half or so of *Religio Laici* reveals, according to a recent account, "that Dryden's arguments form a coherent sequence of ideas in which each principal stage of the discourse depends on the one which immediately precedes it. Thus, his demonstration of the necessity of revelation leads to the question of where this revelation is to be found, and his affirmation that it is contained in the Bible leads to a consideration of the objection to this theory";[15] these arguments Dryden seems to have taken from Sir Charles Wolseley's *The Reasonableness of Scripture-Belief* (1672). In any case, lines 1–125 have been reduced to a straightforward demonstration of the "inadequacy of natural religion" (ll. 1–92) and of our "dependence on revelation for the means of atonement" (ll. 93–125).[16] Now it is undeniable that these arguments may be extracted from the poem because Dryden has relied on apologetical works in making his poem, but to remove these arguments from their poetic context in this literalist fashion, ignoring the means by which they are made and the ends they are designed to serve, is to distort their intended meaning.

The primary goal of *Religio Laici*, its fundamental direction, and its precise—indeed, unique—status as a layman's faith can, I think, be glimpsed in the magnificent opening eleven lines.

Sometimes read as a subtle rendering of the temporal stages in mankind's accessibility to the knowledge needed for salvation,[17] these lines declare immediately, succinctly, and unequivocally the need to look upward, away from ourselves and our limited reason, to God.

> Dim, as the borrow'd beams of Moon and Stars
> To _lonely, weary, wandring_ Travellers,
> Is _Reason_ to the _Soul:_ And as on high,
> Those rowling Fires _discover_ but the Sky
> Not light us _here;_ So _Reason's_ glimmering Ray ⎫
> Was lent, not to _assure_ our _doubtfull_ way,   ⎬
> But _guide_ us upward to a _better Day._   ⎭
> And as those nightly Tapers disappear
> When Day's bright Lord ascends our Hemisphere;
> So pale grows _Reason_ at _Religions_ sight;
> So _dyes,_ and so _dissolves_ in _Supernatural Light._

At the outset, with traditional metaphors, Dryden affirms reason's limited power, thus demarcating a middle ground distinct from both the fideism with which Bredvold linked him and the rationalism with which Budick and others have recently associated him. Reason's "Ray," though necessary, is only "glimmering" and "lent." That is, even such a faculty as the reason, the highest in man, which we ordinarily believe to be merely natural, is in truth of divine origin and a gift from God, which we are ultimately to surrender. The job of reason is to "_guide_ us upward," and this the poem too undertakes to do. The point is repeated several times in various ways (e.g., "Look humbly upward," l. 101; "sadly are we sure / _Still_ to be _Sick,_ till _Heav'n_ reveal the _Cure,_" ll. 119–20) and dramatized in the verses immediately following the exordium.

We can better understand Dryden's position if we now compare the exordium with a structurally similar passage in a book that he probably knew well and may even have been attempting to answer. That is _A Treatise of Humane Reason,_ written by Martin

Clifford, master of the Charterhouse, a collaborator on *The Rehearsal*, and a long-standing foe of Dryden.[18] The publication of this tract in 1674 touched off a "serious crisis of authority" within the Church of England[19] and provoked numerous replies as late as the 1680s. Whether or not *Religio Laici* contributed to this controversy, its positions appear in bold relief against the background provided by Clifford's book.

To begin with, Dryden's imagery is the same as Clifford's, and the goal they seek is the same. Like Lord Herbert in his layman's faith, Clifford opens with the shop-worn picture of *"lonely, weary, wandring* Travellers" going through life, searching for happiness and "some Guide, for so long and so dangerous a journey." The guide soon found is, as in Dryden's *Religio Laici,* the traveler's own reason. As he continues, now employing the familiar light imagery with which Dryden later constructed his own opening, the differences, already suggested in the autonomy Clifford gives to reason, emerge fully. Those who oppose reason as man's necessary and sufficient guide, he declares, much like the authors of layman's faiths, "seek to terrifie us with the example of many excellent Wits, who, they say, by following this *Ignis fatuus* (for so they call the only *North-Star* which God has given us for the right Steering of our course) have fallen into wild and ridiculous Opinions, and encreased the catalogue of Heresies to so vast a number."[20] Clifford denies that unrestricted use of the reason produced such errors and insists on the advantages "if this doctrine of governing our selves from within . . . were establisht. Whereas on the contrary side, the submitting our judgments to Authority, or any thing else whatsoever, gives universality and perpetuity to every error." Flouting the ultimate submissiveness that Dryden extols, Clifford claims that the needed light is already within the human breast, not outside, above, and beyond man: "we say that every mans Soul hath in it self as much light as is requisite for our travel towards Heaven"; unlike the Cambridge Platonists, who similarly adopt an innatist position, he never suggests that this inner light must be triggered by God. Though couched in similar language, the controlling principles of Dryden and Clifford are polar opposites, for whereas Dryden would "*guide* us upward," his longtime enemy would turn us inward: "The ordinary saying of *Democritus* that *Truth lyes in the bottom of a deep Well,* is very applicable to this matter: that is, that we must seek it in the center and heart of our selves, and not look up into Heaven first and immediately for it; because by this means we shall see Heaven in the bottom of the Well, though we could not the Well in the top of Heaven." [21] In Dryden's terms, as stated in the Preface to *Religio Laici,* Clifford is one of those who "have too much exalted the faculties of our Souls." Dryden's contention, first stated in the Preface, then repeated in the exordium, and implied throughout the poem, that "we have not lifted up our selves to God, by the weak Pinions of our Reason, but he has been pleasd to descend to us" seems a pointed response to Clifford's internalization of authority and casts doubt on recent attempts to align Dryden with the Cambridge Platonists and the later Latitudinarians.

Clifford proceeds to develop the individualist religious and political implications of his premise, Dryden to validate dramatically his argument for Ultimate Authority, demonstrating the way in which reason leads us to rely on the power, justice, and mercy of God and revealing the poem's divergence from other layman's faiths, which were by and large antiauthoritarian. To illustrate his argument that reason must eventually be self-consuming, Dryden first provides a historical account of man's search for the secrets of human life.

> Some few, whose Lamp shone brighter, have been led
> From Cause to Cause, to *Natures* secret head;
> And found that *one first principle* must be.
>
> (ll. 12–14)

Because not even the wisest of those early men was able to determine the nature of that mysterious force, Dryden can point to the relative powerlessness of man when dependent upon only his own unaided abilities—and so lay a trap for the Deist.

But *what*, or *who*, that UNIVERSAL HE;
Whether some *Soul* incompassing this Ball
Unmade, unmov'd; yet *making, moving All;*
Or various *Atoms* interfering Dance
Leapt into *Form*, (the noble work of *Chance;*)
Or this great *All* was from *Eternity;* ⎫
Not ev'n the *Stagirite* himself could see; ⎬
And *Epicurus Guess'd* as well as He: ⎭
As *blindly grop'd* they for a *future State;*
As *rashly Judg'd* of *Providence* and *Fate.*

(ll. 15–24)

In the related attempt to discover the requirements of happiness, the pagans were even less successful:

But least of all could their Endeavours find
What most concern'd the good of Humane kind:
For *Happiness* was never to be found;
But vanish'd from 'em, like Enchanted ground.
One thought *Content* the Good to be enjoy'd:
This, every little *Accident* destroy'd:
The *wiser Madmen* did for *Vertue* toyl:
A Thorny, or at best a barren Soil:
In *Pleasure* some their glutton Souls would steep; ⎫
But found their Line too short, the Well too deep; ⎬
And leaky Vessels which no *Bliss* cou'd keep. ⎭

(ll. 25–35)

In the final lines of this long opening verse paragraph Dryden's tone becomes even sharper and more sarcastic as he trumpets the point at least implicit all along. God is inscrutable to inferior, dependent man, who requires help from beyond himself if he is to find the elusive "Summum Bonum":

Thus, *anxious Thoughts* in *endless Circles* roul,
Without a *Centre* where to fix the *Soul:*
In this wilde Maze their vain Endeavours end:

> How can the *less* the *Greater* comprehend?
> Or *finite Reason* reach *Infinity?*
> For what cou'd *Fathom GOD* were *more* than *He.*
>   (ll. 36–41)

Dryden now turns to the Deist as one who supposes he has found the answers to age-old questions. The picture drawn is poetically important and historically accurate in particulars.

> The Deist thinks he stands on firmer ground;
> Cries ἐυρηκα: the mighty Secret's found:
> *God* is that *Spring* of *Good; Supreme,* and *Best;*
> *We,* made to *serve,* and in that Service *blest;*
> If so, some *Rules* of Worship must be given,
> Distributed alike to all by Heaven:
> Else *God* were *partial,* and to *some* deny'd
> The Means his Justice shou'd for *all* provide.[22]
> This *general Worship* is to PRAISE, and PRAY:
> One part to *borrow* Blessings, one to *pay:*
> And when frail Nature slides into *Offence,*
> The *Sacrifice* for *Crimes* is *Penitence.*
> Yet, since th' Effects of Providence, we find
> Are variously dispens'd to Humane kind;
> That *Vice Triumphs,* and *Vertue suffers* here,
> (A Brand that Sovereign Justice cannot bear;)
> Our Reason prompts us to a *future* State:
> The *last Appeal* from *Fortune,* and from *Fate:*
> Where God's all-righteous ways will be declar'd;
> The *Bad* meet *Punishment,* the *Good, Reward.*
>   (ll. 42–61)

By more than one means this first speech by an *adversarius* exposes the Deist's pride and presumption. Unlike apologists for Christianity, Dryden's opponent employs the usual Deistic method of reasoning, which was "to deduce the being and attributes of God *a priori* from 'the nature and reason of things' and then from God's attributes to deduce man's religious and moral duties."[23] The defenders of Christianity, who argued *a posteriori*, rejected this "idle and visionary" manner of reasoning downward from one's own hypothesis regarding the divine attributes because predicated, Clifford-like, on "the *sufficiency*, and *absolute perfection*, of the light and strength of human reason."[24] As Dryden depicts him, the Deist imposes his own rationally conceived expectations on God; that is, when, because "*Vice Triumphs*, and *Vertue suffers* here," the Deist is prompted by his reason to infer that "a *future* State" must exist in order to correct injustice, he is not only claiming knowledge of what man cannot know but in effect dictating to God. Overstepping his bounds, the Deist becomes "*more* than *He*": "Thus Man by his own strength to Heaven wou'd soar: / And wou'd not be Oblig'd to God for more" (ll. 62–63). The point is repeated, in terms that establish the political implications, in lines 93–98.

The reason for the Deist's relatively greater success in the search for human happiness, already indicated in the Preface, is that, unlike the Ancients, he enjoys the benefits of revelation. Thus what appear to be "God-like Notions" (l. 65) arrived at by the Deist's unaided natural powers actually derive from God.

> These Truths are not the product of thy Mind,
> But dropt from Heaven, and of a Nobler kind.
> *Reveal'd Religion* first inform'd thy Sight,
> And *Reason* saw not, till *Faith* sprung the Light.
> (ll. 66–69)

Properly employing reason, Dryden undercuts the Deist's vain belief in reason's sufficiency:

> 'Tis *Revelation* what thou thinkst *Discourse*.
> Else, how com'st *Thou* to see these truths so clear,
> Which so obscure to *Heathens* did appear?
> Not *Plato* these, nor *Aristotle* found:
> Nor He whose Wisedom *Oracles* renown'd.
> Hast thou a Wit so deep, or so sublime,
> Or canst thou lower dive, or higher climb?

> Canst *Thou,* by *Reason,* more of *God-head* know
> Than *Plutarch, Seneca,* or *Cicero?*
>
> (ll. 71–79)

Having treated the Deist primarily for illustrative purposes in an argument begun well before he was introduced,[25] Dryden now proceeds with his central concern, the "Summum Bonum" and the way in which human happiness is inseparable from proper relationship to God. Man need only "Look humbly upward" and depend on *"Eternal Wisedom,"* which opens doors otherwise sealed to finite man. The tone remains satirical, the aim being, like Pope's in *An Essay on Man,* to elevate the Deity at presumptuous man's expense.

> . . . if there be a *Pow'r* too *Just* and *strong*
> To wink at *Crimes,* and bear unpunish'd *Wrong;*
> Look humbly upward, see his Will disclose
> The *Forfeit* first, and then the *Fine* impose:
> A *Mulct thy* Poverty cou'd never pay
> Had not *Eternal Wisedom* found the way
> And with Cœlestial Wealth supply'd thy Store:
> *His Justice* makes the *Fine,* his *Mercy* quits the *Score.*
> See God descending in thy Humane Frame;
> Th' *offended,* suff'ring in th' *Offenders* Name:
> All thy Misdeeds to him imputed see,
> And all his Righteousness devolv'd on thee.
>
> (ll. 99–110)

Reason is responsible for this insight:

> For granting we have Sin'd, and that th' offence
> Of *Man,* is made against *Omnipotence,*
> Some Price, that bears *proportion,* must be paid;
> And *Infinite* with *Infinite* be weigh'd.
> See then the *Deist lost: Remorse* for *Vice,*
> *Not* paid, or *paid, inadequate* in price:

What farther means can *Reason* now direct,
Or what Relief from *humane Wit* expect?
That shews us *sick;* and sadly are we sure
Still to be *Sick,* till *Heav'n* reveal the *Cure:*
If then *Heaven's Will* must needs be understood,
(Which must, if we want *Cure,* and *Heaven* be *Good)*
Let all Records of *Will reveal'd* be shown; ⎫
With *Scripture,* all in equal ballance thrown, ⎬
And *our one Sacred Book* will be *That one.* ⎭

(ll. 111–25)

Having guided us upward to God as the source of human good and to the need to know his Will if we are to approach happiness, Dryden now argues that Scripture is that *"Will reveal'd."* He offers as support a series of six moral arguments (ll. 126–67), which appear to be collected haphazardly, creating "the impression that he is choosing at random from among dozens" of convincing possibilities.[26] Here too Dryden expects reason to lead us to the truth that Heaven directed the writers of Scripture. He concludes this rather Horatian section with a restatement of his principal point:

To what can *Reason* such Effects assign
Transcending *Nature,* but to *Laws Divine?*
Which in that Sacred Volume are contain'd;
Sufficient, clear, and for that use ordain'd.

(ll. 164–67)

At this point Dryden presents the major Deistic objection that the revelation described in Scripture cannot be valid because supernatural and therefore partial, not universal. According to Dryden, "Of all Objections this indeed is chief / To startle Reason, stagger frail Belief" (ll. 184–85):

But stay: the *Deist* here will urge anew,
No *Supernatural Worship* can be *True:*

> Because a *general Law* is that alone
> Which must to *all,* and *every where* be known:
> A Style so large as not *this* Book can claim
> Nor ought that bears *reveal'd* Religions *Name.*
> 'Tis said the sound of a *Messiah's Birth*
> Is gone through all the habitable Earth:
> But still that Text must be confin'd alone
> To what was *Then* inhabited, and known:
> And what Provision cou'd from *thence* accrue
> To *Indian* Souls, and Worlds discovered *New?*
> In other parts it helps, that, Ages past,
> The Scriptures there were *known,* and were *imbrac'd,*
> Till Sin spread once again the Shades of Night:
> What's that to these who never *saw* the Light?
>   (ll. 168–83)

A moment of some importance in the poem, this objection and Dryden's response dramatically validate another point stated in the exordium. Relying completely on abstract reason, the Deist denies himself access to God's "*Will reveal'd*" to mankind because there is no satisfactory rational answer to his question. "With how much more plausibility of Reason [any heresy] combats our Religion," Dryden had warned in the Preface, "with so much more caution [it is] to be avoided." Properly employed, its limits respected, reason grows pale "at *Religions* sight; / So *dyes,* and so *dissolves* in *Supernatural Light.*" Therefore, accepting his own inability to answer the Deist's pointed question and respecting God's inscrutability, Dryden places in him his hopes for those living before or beyond the reach of the Gospel.

> We grant, 'tis true, that Heav'n from humane Sense
> Has hid the secret paths of *Providence:*
> But *boundless Wisedom, boundless Mercy,* may
> Find ev'n for those *be-wildred* Souls, a *way:*
> If from his *Nature Foes* may Pity claim,
> Much more may *Strangers* who ne'er heard his *Name.*
> And though *no Name* be for *Salvation* known,

But that of his *Eternal Sons* alone;
Who knows how far transcending Goodness can
Extend the *Merits* of *that Son* to *Man?*
Who knows what *Reasons* may his *Mercy* lead;
Or *Ignorance invincible* may plead? [27]

(ll. 186–97)

Whereas the Deist forgoes Scripture in order to maintain his reason inviolate, Dryden is willing to dissolve his reason in his faith. If momentarily "staggered," Dryden remains true to the position assumed from the beginning but until now unchallenged.

Missing Dryden's aim in *Religio Laici,* signaled in the exordium and developed in later verses, commentators have failed to grasp the meaning and significance of his treatment of Deism, Catholicism, and sectarianism. Ordinarily, on the basis of a literal reading, Dryden's interest has been said to lie in those positions per se. Such a reading fails, I think, to take sufficient account of *Religio Laici* as poetry.

Dryden borrows from Horace the device of *adversarius,* making the Deist and the two Catholic speakers representatives and embodiments of the doctrines they profess (that sectarianism is not allowed a direct advocate attests to both Dryden's low estimate of it religiously and the relatively great danger he sees in it). That Dryden confronts the proponents of these religious positions is itself important, suggesting the moral, rather than ecclesiastical, basis of his concern. But more important is the subtle way in which Dryden transforms into poetry the apologetics on which he has drawn, a transformation clearest in the depiction of his opponents. The quality of Dryden's stylistic effort in *Religio Laici* is reflected in the poem's self-consciousness, passages strategically placed at the beginning, middle, and end reflexively insisting that the work is poetry.[28] Ultimately, Dryden's effort is not much below the brilliant metaphorical success of *Absalom and Achitophel.* The mode is in fact similar to that of the earlier, political poem, though more strik-

ing if less appreciated. Here, too, the real subject, implied in the
stated effort to "*guide* us upward," is an abstract, general theme,
achieved through the use of the Deist and the Catholics as metaphors; they represent general moral concepts and serve as the
vehicles of Dryden's meaning. Significantly, that meaning is explicitly stated at the conclusion of the discussions with the
adversarii.

> So all we make of Heavens discover'd Will
> Is, not to have it, or to use it ill.
> The Danger's much the same; on several Shelves
> If *others* wreck *us*, or *we* wreck our *selves.*
>
> What then remains, but, waving each Extreme,
> The Tides of Ignorance, and Pride to stem:
> Neither so rich a Treasure to forgo;
> Nor proudly seek beyond our pow'r to know?
>   (ll. 423–30)

The Deist, by means of the obstructing mediation of im-
properly employed reason, would not accept Scripture as "*This
one Rule of Life*" all men need; he thus exemplifies self-destruc-
tion, as do, in somewhat different fashion, the sectarians, who
effectively deny themselves access to that saving rule. The Catholics, on the other hand, represent the situation whereby "*others
wreck us,*" attempting to keep Scripture from the laity. Ultimately, however, all three positions are variations on a single
theme, directly contrasted with the proper mode of the poet
himself. For if in one sense "ignorance" seems most appropriate
for the plight of the layman under Catholic domination, "pride"
appears in all three opponents. But in another sense both pride
and ignorance characterize all three, for the Deist, the Catholics,
and the sectarians remain essentially ignorant of Scripture because, in their respective ways, they all proudly forgo God's
Holy Word.[29] Let us look now at the Catholics and the sectarians, who appear in the second half of the poem, where the
issue is the proper means by which the layman should approach
Scripture, previously established as "*our one Sacred Book.*"

We might expect Dryden to stress common grounds between the Deist and sectarians, for both locate the source of authority within man, the Deist relying on reason, the sectarians on the "private spirit." But to argue the recurrence of the Deist's fundamental error in different, subtler form in the Catholic position is daring and unexpected. Yet this is exactly what Dryden does, responding to a Catholic objection, voiced by an unidentified *adversarius*, that

> . . . since th' *original* Scripture has been lost,
> *All* Copies *disagreeing, maim'd* the *most*,
> Or *Christian Faith* can have no *certain* ground,
> Or *Truth* in *Church Tradition* must be found.
> (ll. 278–81)

Dryden's ingenious reply equates the traditional claim to infallibility in morals and matters of faith with omniscience; he begins with obvious irony: [30]

> Such an *Omniscient* Church we wish indeed;
> 'Twere worth *Both Testaments*, and cast in the *Creed:*
> But if *this Mother* be a *Guid* so sure,
> As can all *doubts resolve*, all *truth secure*,
> Then her *Infallibility*, as well
> Where Copies are *corrupt*, or *lame*, can tell;
> Restore *lost Canon* with as little pains,
> As *truly explicate* what still *remains:*
> Which yet no *Council* dare *pretend* to doe; ⎫
> Unless like *Esdras*, they cou'd *write* it new: ⎬
> Strange Confidence, still to *interpret* true, ⎭
> Yet not be sure that all they have explain'd,
> Is in the blest *Original* contain'd.
> (ll. 282–94)

Rather than willfully misrepresenting the Catholic position (no apologist ever claimed the church was omniscient), Dryden is here attempting to draw out the implications of the great au-

thority Catholics place in their church, linking her with power
properly resting in God alone. If reason is the final authority for
the Deist, the church occupies that position for the Catholic.
Dryden's answer, directed to both the *adversarius* and the major
problem posed by the *Critical History*,[31] thus corresponds exactly
to the reply offered to the Deist:

> More Safe, and much more modest 'tis, to say
> *God wou'd not leave Mankind without a way:*
> And that the *Scriptures*, though not *every where*
> Free from Corruption, or intire, or clear,
> Are uncorrupt, sufficient, clear, intire,
> In *all* things which our needfull *Faith* require.
>
> (ll. 295–300)

Dryden's appeal to Providence here, echoing the point of *The
Spanish Fryar*, is most important. He implicitly opposes Providence and the church, which he has already implicated in "*Interest*" and "*Gain*" (l. 275), the former presented as a direct
antithesis of the Christian religion ("This *onely* Doctrine" works
"Cross to our *Interests*," ll. 158, 160), and claims that no matter
how many corruptions may be found in Scripture, those texts
remain "uncorrupt, sufficient, clear, intire, / In *all* things which
our needfull *Faith* require" because "*God wou'd not leave Mankind
without a way.*" This reliance on Providence Dryden describes as
"much more modest," implying a contrasting pride in the Catholics' final appeal to an institution that is of merely human constitution if of divine origin.

Later on Dryden is even more direct in illustrating the way
the Catholics represent a position that would "wreck" us by mediating our access to Scripture and imposing the word of the
church on God's Word. His most vehement assault on the clergy
in the poem, as well as his most substantial treatment of the
Catholic mode of usurping the power and place of God, this
passage reflects the oppositions characteristic of the layman's
faith tradition. The commercial imagery enforces the earlier linking of the church with "*Gain*."

In times o'ergrown with Rust and Ignorance,
A gainfull Trade their Clergy did advance:
When want of Learning kept the *Laymen* low,
And none but *Priests* were *Authoriz'd* to *know:*
When what small Knowledge was, in them did dwell;
And he a *God* who cou'd but *Reade* or *Spell;*
Then *Mother Church* did mightily prevail:
She parcel'd out the Bible by *retail:*
But still *expounded* what She *sold* or *gave;*
To keep it in *her Power* to *Damn* and *Save:*
Scripture was *scarce,* and as the Market went,
Poor *Laymen* took *Salvation* on *Content;*
As needy men take Money, good or bad:
God's Word they had not, but the *Priests* they had.
Yet, whate'er *false Conveyances* they made,
The *Lawyer* still was *certain* to be paid.
In those dark times they learn'd their knack so well,
That by long use they grew *Infallible:*
At last, a knowing Age began t' enquire
If *they* the *Book,* or *That* did *them* inspire:
And, making narrower search they found, thô late,
That what they thought the *Priest*'s, was *Their* Estate:
Taught by the *Will produc'd,* (the written Word)
How long they had been *cheated* on *Record.* [32]

(ll. 370–93)

As a result of the Reformation, the laity rightly enjoyed unmediated access to God's Word. But "This good had full as bad a
Consequence" (l. 399). Freed from the priestly tyranny which
spelled their destruction, Protestant laymen, overreaching their
bounds and newly mediating the texts for which they had
fought, now proceeded to "wreck" themselves. Suggested in
the fact that line 389 ("If *they* the *Book,* or *That* did *them* inspire"), referring to Catholics, closely echoes a line in *The Medall*
on "Fanatick" manipulation of Scripture ("The Text inspires not
them; but they the Text inspire," l. 166), Dryden sees this event
as fundamentally like the Catholic error;[33] in both positions, as

well as in the Deist's, appears the antithesis of the theme an-
nounced in the exordium and developed thereafter. The danger
is much the same with Catholicism and sectarianism. Because in
both cases the Bible is not allowed to *"speak . . . it Self"* (l. 368),
it is man, not God, who emerges in every line of interpreted
Scripture, whether the "expounding" is done by church or private individual with the aid of the "spirit." If under Catholic
domination the layman was prohibited access to Scripture, with
the tyranny of the spirit he is "free" of the Bible.

> The Book thus put in every vulgar hand,
> Which each presum'd he best cou'd understand,
> The *Common Rule* was made the *common Prey;*
> And at the mercy of the *Rabble* lay.
> The tender Page with horney Fists was gaul'd;
> And he was gifted most that loudest baul'd:
> The *Spirit* gave the *Doctoral Degree:* ⎫
> And every member of a *Company*   ⎬
> Was of *his Trade,* and of the *Bible free.* ⎭
> Plain *Truths* enough for needfull *use* they found;
> But men wou'd still be itching to *expound:*
> Each was ambitious of th' obscurest place,
> No measure ta'n from *Knowledge,* all from GRACE.
> *Study* and *Pains* were now no more their Care;
> *Texts* were explain'd by *Fasting,* and by *Prayer.*
>   (ll. 400–414)

The center of *Religio Laici* is the pride the poet rejects and attempts to overcome as he *"guide*[s] us upward," as well as the
kinds of ignorance manifest in the layman's tyrannization by a
proud clergy and in the distance from God's Holy Word resulting from various prideful mediations on Scripture.

The end of *Religio Laici* is deliberately low key and plain, in
contrast with the highly poetic and moving opening. The penultimate verse paragraph, which begins this modulation to
those final six verses, is, of course, the conclusion to the argu-

ment, though it hardly seems a conclusion at all. This is due in part to the fact that Dryden, writing in the layman's faith tradition, believes that if once the errors of pride and ignorance are removed, the ecclesiastical contours of what remains are of little moment; thus the conclusion of both argument and poem can appear relatively unimportant, if not actually self-effacing.

> What then remains, but, waving each Extreme,
> The Tides of Ignorance, and Pride to stem:
> Neither so rich a Treasure to forgo;
> Nor proudly seek beyond our pow'r to know?
>
> (ll. 426–30)

The particular nature of this conclusion derives as well from the fact that the desired alternative to the dangerous extremes represented in the Deist, the Catholics, and the sectarians, a moral and theological stance, cannot be so much conceptualized as exemplified. That alternative, rightly excited by errors, follies, and vices, rather than by minute institutional differences, and devoted to the correction of abuses instead of the promulgation of a specific path, has been apparent from the very beginning and so now need only be briefly summarized. Dryden strives to embody in the character of himself projected in the poem the moral norms of that work, notably a freedom to treat of "Sacred things" tempered with a judicious sense of religious and civil responsibility, a just suspicion of merely private opinion alongside an artful disciplining of the fallen will, a becoming submissiveness to Ultimate Authority that insures that he will "lay no unhallow'd hand upon the Ark." In short, neither proud nor ignorant, Dryden embodies the desired alternative.

Rather than arguing for one true church, therefore, *Religio Laici*, in the manner characteristic of layman's faiths, not only forgoes a plea for any particular church but seems in fact to minimize the power, role, and need of ecclesiastical institutions in general. Dryden is not altogether successful, therefore, in avoiding the individualism his poem is designed to combat. The bold and daring representation of the Catholic Church as aspiring to, and indeed usurping, the authority of God bears generalized implications, for that church represents a situation whereby "*others* wreck *us.*" Throughout Dryden opposes any mediation between man and God. Thus he not only asserts the individual's responsibility to believe for himself in matters of religion,

> If *others* in the *same Glass better* see
> 'Tis for *Themselves* they look, but not for *me:*
> For MY Salvation must its Doom receive
> Not from what OTHERS, but what I believe.
>   (ll. 301–4)

but he also insists on absolute adherence to the fundamental Protestant principle of *Scriptura sola.* In perhaps the clearest single expression of his carefully established position, Dryden asks whether the Catholics can legitimately conclude from the fact that they are the transmitters of Scripture

> A right t' interpret? or wou'd they alone
> Who brought the Present, claim it for their own?
> The *Book's* a *Common Largess* to *Mankind;*
> Not more for *them,* than *every* Man design'd:
> The *welcome News* is in the *Letter* found;
> The *Carrier's* not Commission'd to *expound.*
> It *speaks* it *Self,* and what it does contain,
> In all things *needfull* to be *known,* is *plain.*
>   (ll. 362–69)

Employing the Protestant argument of John Tillotson that "Our Principle is, That the Scripture doth sufficiently interpret it self, that is, is plain to all capacities, in things necessary to be believed and practised" and of the Dissenter Henry Care that "The Infallible Rule of the Interpretation of Scripture is the Scripture it self," Dryden makes interpretation supererogatory.[34]

Besides including the church in the sweeping condemnation of impositions on God's Ultimate Authority, Dryden's trumpeted stress on *Scriptura sola,* viewed in its poetic context and that of Dryden's thought generally, and considered alongside his repeated opposition to "expounding," whether by individual or church, Catholic or Protestant, and his formulation that Scripture *"speaks it Self,"* seems to obviate the need of the church as guide and mediator. For as the author of *Two Letters of Advice, I. For the Susception of Holy Orders. II. For Studies Theological* observed, understood radically *Scriptura sola* deprives "the *Clergie* of the *Authority* even of *proponents,* which is the least that can be imagined, and therefore must needs degrade them to an *equality* with the *Laity* . . . the *Laity* now conceiving themselves as *Adversaries* concerned to maintain their *Liberty* against the *conceived usurpations of the Clergie."*[35] According to the anonymous author of *The Several Ways of Resolving Faith,* moreover, this principle is not only destructive of church authority but individualistic in the extreme: it sets up "a *Pope* in every private mans breast," making him "certainly *infallible* in that wherein he cannot unless he will himself, be deceiv'd."[36] But if the means Dryden employs are susceptible to such an untraditional and individualistic effect, in his hands they are directed toward quite different, indeed completely conventional, ends.[37] As a matter of fact, lines 305–55, the *"Objection in behalf of Tradition; urg'd by Father* Simon" and Dryden's reply, represent an attempt to clarify his position so as to distinguish it precisely from the kind of thought with which it might be associated on a cursory reading, that is, to separate it from any desire to set up the private individual in the "Papal Chair," an attempt both he and the author of *The Several Ways of Resolving Faith* vigorously resist. Creech was exactly right when he declared in his introductory poem to *Religio Laici* that Dryden "freest us from a double Care, / The bold Socinian, and the Papal Chair," avoiding the extreme to which the effort to secure lay independence of the clergy could lead—and did in Lord Herbert and others.

Following Dryden's strident Protestant assertion of the need of unmediated access to God, Father Simon understandably wants to know, "Must *all Tradition* then be set aside?" He adds, in the same terms Dryden uses in the penultimate verse paragraph, "This to affirm were Ignorance, or Pride" (l. 307). Thus claiming for his position the very virtues Dryden appropriates for his, the priest argues that scriptural obscurity is not limited to passages "concluded not necessary to be known." Putting Dryden on the defensive and necessitating an exact delineation and eventually a refinement of position, this *adversarius* repeats the poet's own claim, made variously at the time, that many of these obscure points, "some needfull sure / To saving Faith" "every Sect will wrest a several way / (For what *one* Sect Interprets, *all* Sects *may*)" (ll. 307–10), his aim being to establish the need of the church as *"unerring Guid."* Against *Scriptura sola* he tellingly notes the considerable disagreement expressed over the central point of the Christian religion by those who insist, like Dryden, that Scripture *"speaks* it *Self,* and what it does contain, / In all things *needfull* to be *known,* is *plain."*

> We hold, and say we prove from Scripture plain, ⎫
> That *Christ* is GOD; the bold *Socinian* ⎬
> From the *same* Scripture urges he's but MAN. ⎭
> Now what appeal can end th' important Suit?
> *Both* parts *talk* loudly, but the *Rule* is *mute.*
>
> (ll. 311–15)

Dryden responds:

> Shall I speak plain, and in a Nation free[38]
> Assume an honest *Layman's Liberty?*
> I think (according to my little Skill,)
> (To my own Mother-Church submitting still)
> That many have been sav'd, and many may,
> Who never heard this Question brought in play.
> Th' *unletter'd* Christian, who believes in *gross,*
> Plods on to *Heaven;* and ne'er is at a loss:
> For the *Streight-gate* wou'd be made *streighter* yet,
> Were *none* admitted there but men of *Wit.*
> The few, by Nature form'd, with Learning fraught,
> Born to instruct, as others to be taught,

Must Study well the Sacred Page; and see
Which Doctrine, this, or that, does best agree
With the whole Tenour of the Work Divine:
And plainlyest points to Heaven's reveal'd Design:
Which Exposition flows from *genuine Sense;*
And which is *forc'd* by *Wit* and *Eloquence.*

(ll. 316–33)

In order to argue that *Scriptura sola* need not result in the manipulation and abuse that have so often accompanied its adoption, Dryden is forced by Father Simon to distinguish between the responsibilities of the ordinary layman, which is simply to believe "in *gross*" and certainly not to concern himself with unnecessary details, and specialists, biblical scholars, to whom alone falls the task of scrupulously examining minutiae and struggling to clarify the various ambiguities present. This emphasis on "*gross*" belief seems to leave no room for concern with the doctrinal differences that separate churches from one another. At any rate, unlike those Protestants, Anglican and Dissenting both, who urged all men to "search the Scriptures,"[39] Dryden counsels the post-Reformation layman to use his freedom and opportunity wisely and responsibly, to exercise self-restraint, and willingly to forgo the "itching to *expound*" that has followed upon unlimited access to "*This one Rule of Life.*" Moreover, just as earlier he juxtaposed Providence and the church, so here he contrasts the power of church tradition with that of Scripture itself,[40] reasserting the claim (ll. 121–67) that Scripture is accepted as "*our one Sacred Book*" on its intrinsic merit, not because of church authority. Written tradition, he maintains, more authoritative than oral,

. . . as perfect as its kind can be,
Rouls down to us the Sacred History:
Which, from the *Universal Church receiv'd,*
Is *try'd,* and *after,* for its *self* believ'd.

(ll. 352–55)

With a unique treatment of *Scriptura sola* Dryden thus exploits the antiecclesiasticism inherent in the principle while upholding Ultimate Authority, cleverly diverting to the church the blame often placed on the proponents of that principle and avoiding the conclusion many thought would follow from opposition to the priesthood.[41] Dryden minimizes the church not in order to set up "a *Pope* in every private mans breast" but only to elevate the Ultimate Authority which is God alone. Dryden's position, therefore, would eliminate the dangerous abuse of Scripture, at the hands of laity and clergy alike, without requiring that the layman relinquish the freedom given him by the Reformation. It is a compromise and tenuous suggestion.

Moreover, it will be observed that in beginning his reply to Father Simon Dryden shifts the grounds of discussion from the priest's particular question to the quite different and broader issue of the core of belief essential for salvation. Poetically useful in the long run, this maneuver blankets, and tends to obscure, Dryden's recognition, perhaps fleeting and quickly repressed, that *Scriptura sola* is vulnerable in the way Catholics, Socinians, and others claimed, on the most fundamental question of all, Christ's nature. Though this passage has recently been interpreted as a sign of Dryden's inclination to the rational religion of the Deist and the Socinian,[42] there is not the slightest hint of doubt, so far as I can see, regarding the divinity of Christ. What these verses reveal, instead, is Dryden's failure, indeed powerlessness, to deny that even such passages in Scripture as those treating of Christ's nature are obscure. In shunting Father Simon's query Dryden demonstrates, no doubt unconsciously, that for him at least Scripture alone is not able to settle all necessary questions and cannot, therefore, serve as the necessary final judge and arbiter of disputes.

Surely no part of Dryden's intention, this revelation, once understood, likely had no small effect on his decision within a few years to convert to the church of his priestly *adversarius*, described in *The Hind and the Panther*, as by Father Simon, as the "unerring Guide" graciously provided by God "For erring judgments" (1:65). His ingenious attempt in *Religio Laici* to resolve his own tensions and at the same time restore "*Common quiet,*"[43] and with it a return to *pietas,* though brilliant poetically, was not adequate.

5

Change and Continuity in Dryden's Conversion

Though few are now likely to question Dryden's sincerity in converting to Roman Catholicism shortly after James's succession in 1685, the motives behind his change of faith remain obscure. For a while, on the basis of Bredvold's attractive argument regarding the development of Dryden's thought from philosophical skepticism to a logical terminus in Catholic fideism, which silenced the charges of expediency vigorously bruited in the nineteenth century,[1] the problem seemed solved. But the overthrow of that influential interpretation in the 1960s has left us with no satisfactory explanation of the reasons for Dryden's conversion. Fortunately this new situation has not revived the familiar charges of time-serving.

Several recent attempts have been made to account for the conversion, but none seems adequate to the complex task. These attempts have taken three main forms. One insists on the primacy of political considerations in Dryden's decision. The fullest expression of this approach is by Donald R. Benson, who has been followed to a degree by Earl Miner and, less cautiously, William Myers.[2] Carefully attending to the political concerns Dryden articulated in various works from the early 1680s through the revolution of 1688, Benson argues that the poet embraced Catholicism when he became convinced that "the Church of England was moving in a political direction opposite from his own" and that only the Church of Rome could restore

"*Common quiet*" and "guarantee the integrity of the Christian Church in England and of English society at large."[3] Though the first point is sound, the second, predicated on the notion that Dryden expected Catholicism again to become the religion of most Englishmen, is not and tends to obscure the genuine value of the former. Moreover, Benson's argument smacks of the discredited charges of the expedient and pragmatic while diminishing the role of the intellectual and religious in Dryden's conversion. Raising this same objection, R. W. McHenry, Jr., has tried to explain the poet's decision differently, in terms of changing assumptions regarding the power of human reason. Recognizing both error and insight in Bredvold's account, McHenry locates in *Religio Laici* a traditionalist use of "right reason," derived from Aquinas by way of Hooker, which contrasts with the "excesses" of reason in Wolseley, whose work Dryden may have drawn on in his layman's faith, and in the Cambridge Platonists. By the time of *The Hind and the Panther*, according to this argument, Dryden had come to believe that "reason is a wholly inadequate foundation for religious doctrine" and was now much disturbed that it had become "the 'private reason' of every man, and as such potentially chaotic and unreliable. . . . These conclusions mean that the Anglican bases for authority have been destroyed, and once they are gone, for a Christian in Dryden's time in England, there remain only two religious creeds—those of the dissenting sects and the Roman Catholic Church."[4] Though attractive in certain respects, this interpretation ignores the potential difficulties raised by Dryden's pre-1677 opinions, barely considers the respective positions and states of Anglicanism and Catholicism in the late seventeenth century, and seems not sufficiently aware of Dryden's militant opposition to the "private reason" as early as *Religio Laici*. Moreover, it shares with the first interpretation an unlikely reductiveness. The third and final form assumed by recent attempts to account for Dryden's conversion is represented by Phillip Harth. Questioning the validity of the methods employed by other scholars, Harth decides, "We must conclude that *The Hind and the Panther* is no more reliable a guide to the religious conversion which it fol-

lowed than are *Religio Laici* and the political writings which preceded that event."[5] He despairs that much light can be shed on
the issue.

We need not, I think, yield to this despair, though we will do
well to follow Harth's caution. The patterns of thought described in the foregoing pages and the nature of Dryden's intellectual and religious desires in the early to mid-1680s, as we
have discerned them, may be of some use in understanding his
conversion, especially when these are related to the actual religiopolitical situation of mid-decade. I am convinced that we
cannot hope to elucidate this controverted matter apart from
awareness of Dryden's relation to both the Church of England
and the Church of Rome as they existed in the 1680s. Thus, any
attempt to account for the conversion solely in terms of changing assumptions regarding abstract ideas like the reason will appear incomplete. For such ideas did not exist independent of, or
isolated from, the prevailing moral, social, and political environ-
ment. To comprehend any phase of Dryden's thought, and especially that of the months just preceding his formal conversion,
we must consider all such factors.

Though resolution of all questions surrounding the conversion seems impossible at this remove, especially in view of the
paucity of direct information available, we may reasonably expect some new light. For Dryden's change of religion, we now
understand, represented a conversion, not from a firm Anglican
faith, but rather from a layman's faith that emphasized freedom
in matters of belief for the individual layman while insisting on a
strong sense of civil and moral responsibility regarding whatever freedom was gained. This militant opposition to priests and
the church as institution in the years immediately preceding his
conversion seems, however, to make all the more enigmatic his
decision to adopt the religion characterized precisely by the
power and authority of the church as organization and widely
considered to be "priest-ridden." But alongside Dryden's effort
at this time to minimize the role of the priesthood and to eliminate any need of a church as mediator and guide appeared an
even more determined effort against dangers from private inter-

pretation of Scripture, the individualism resulting from proliferation of religious sects, and the threats posed by various internalizations of authority.

By the early 1680s, having already undergone a major intellectual conversion, Dryden not only steadfastly supported the Divine Right of kings but also recognized and subscribed to the religious basis of that position, now in its last stages. As a result of recent experiences, no doubt including awareness of the directions understanding was then taking, he formulated and was able to express brilliantly in his poetry a coherent set of beliefs, perhaps best described as reflective of an Ancient sensibility. Predicated on the recognition that man is not the measure of all things, a belief then being challenged by science and in economics, politics, and even religion, this position led Dryden to stress puny but arrogant man's ultimate and lasting contingency and dependence on God. No longer sanguine about man, progress, and the future, he insisted, especially through repeated evocations of parallel history, that his age recall what mankind had always known: pride, self-assertiveness, and the desire for self-sufficiency are the enemy; more than a particular form of government or social organization, they stand in the way of his advance.

This kind of thinking probably finds its closest analogue in the Restoration in Roman Catholicism, with which Dryden had had certain affinities for some time. How those affinities developed and managed finally to overcome Dryden's opposition to priests and churches, an important vestige of his radical Puritan background, it is our task to try to determine.

Dryden was never very close to the church from which he evidently converted. Sir Walter Scott may have been nearer the truth than recent commentators have been willing to admit when he wrote, "Dryden never could be a firm or steady believer in the Church of England's doctrines."[6] Indeed, much of Dryden's disenchantment with and opposition to the clergy and the church in the early and mid-1680s may be attributed to a felt animosity toward his own Church of England. E. S. de Beer has attributed Dryden's increased anticlericalism to a desire for revenge on the Established clergy for denying him ordination,[7] but this possibility lacks substantive support. We may find more probable reasons for Dryden's actions, and for his considering a change of faith to that of Rome, in the state of Anglicanism at this time.

In describing herself from the beginning as a *via media* between Catholicism and extreme Protestantism, the Church of England established moderation as her defining characteristic. In the late seventeenth century she was able, though not without considerable strain, to house High Churchmen, Latitudinarians, and even some verging dangerously close on Deism and free-thinking. Of the various positions then visible within the church, the most prominent was Latitudinarianism, which, generally speaking, sought to accommodate principles inherent in Anglicanism to the directions and apparent needs of an emerging market society. First derisively applied to the Cambridge Platonists, the term *Latitudinarian* was soon extended to other Anglicans as well, "whose onely Religion," it was claimed, "it is to temporize, & transform themselves into any Shape for their Secular interests; and that judge no Doctrine so Saving, as that which obligeth to so complying and condescending a humour, as to become all things to all men, that so by any means they may gain something."[8] Despite eloquent defenders who fought to present the "Latitude-men" in a better light, the definite triumph of Latitudinarianism after 1688, and the work of recent scholars, the term has never quite recovered from the opprobrium with which it was first greeted. It seems clear now, however, that the Latitudinarians of the Restoration, like their Cambridge forebears, were sincere and dedicated Christians, who sought to continue the Reformation, preserve the Established Church, and Christianize a society that looked more and more secular. Self-styled moderates in both religion and politics, the Latitudinarians, who arose amidst the strait-laced spirit of the Commonwealth, sought to insure a genuine Anglican alternative to both fanaticism and Catholic "tyranny." If these men, who included the most famous churchmen of the period, such as Tillotson, Stillingfleet, and Burnet, as well as scientists like Boyle and Newton, contributed to the rise of Deism, as has so often been charged, it was surely no part of their intention.[9] Yet it must be recognized that the Latitudinarians are quite distinct from those High Churchmen who regarded as subversive the forward-looking beliefs and methods of their fellow churchmen.

Analysis of Latitudinarian emphases does much to explain the suspicion and fear with which these men were viewed. Perhaps the most fundamental fact about the Latitudinarians is that they were "followers . . . of the new Philosophy," S. P. (evidently Simon Patrick) sarcastically noting in their defense that this is a "crime which cannot be denied, that they have introduced a new Philosophy; *Aristotle* and the Schoolemen are out of request with them. True indeed it is that *ipse dixit* is an argument much out of fashion."[10] Adopting the freedom of inquiry and antidogmatism characteristic of the new science, but, according to Joseph Glanvill, bounding "it with so much Caution, that no Prejudice could arise to Legal Establishments from that freedom," the men of Latitude sought to free their own and other minds "from the *Prepossessions,* and *Prejudices* of *Complexion, Education,* and implicit *Authority;* Asserting the Liberty of Enquiry, and thereby freeing their Reasons from a base and dishonourable Servitude, and vindicating this just Right of Humane Nature."[11] In opposition to the tyrannical exclusivism of the sects, as well as the dogmatism of Rome, men, or at least the mature, literate, and judicious, were taught "to *try all things,* as Scripture and Reason require, and incourage us; and to suspend the giving up our *full,* and resolv'd assent to the Doctrines we have been taught, till we have impartially consider'd and examin'd them *our* selves."[12] As one defender put it, "They will certainly unshakle, and disintangle mens minds and give them their due liberty; they will enlarge and widen their Souls, and make them in an excellent and most commendable sense, men of Latitude."[13]

Labeled "the rational preachers," as well as "the moral preachers," the Latitudinarians worked to demonstrate the reasonableness of the Christian religion, maintaining that "Reason *proves some* Main and Fundamental Articles of *Faith*, and *defends all*, by proving the Authority of Holy Scripture." [14] Their reason taught them, says Glanvill, that "Religion, which was *shaken* by *divisions*, and rendered *suspected* of *uncertainty* through the *mixture* of *uncertain* things, would stand *safe*, and *firm* when 'twas lay'd only upon the *plain, infallible, undoubted* propositions: That holiness would thrive, when Mens zeal was taken off from talking, and disputing against others, and directed inwards to the government of themselves, and the reformation of their own hearts, and lives." [15] Relatively little interested in doctrines as such, reluctant to impute damnable opinions to any man, and prone to found religion "in *doing*," the Latitudinarians were "not at all forward to give a Catalogue of Fundamentals; but instead thereof, content[ed] themselves to tell their Hearers, that it is sufficient for any mans Salvation, that he assent to the truth of the Holy Scriptures, that he carefully endeavour to understand their true meaning, so far as concerns his own duty, and to order his life accordingly. And that he whose Conscience tells him, upon an impartial inquiry into himself, that he doth thus, need not fear that he erreth damnably. But into the number of the Doctrines, they account Fundamentals, they will by no means admit any, that are not plainly revealed." [16]

The Latitude-men taught that the principles of religion necessary to salvation are few, plain, and generally acknowledged because, in Glanvill's words, "they saw it would secure Charity to dissenters" and lessen the risk of further schisms, persecutions, and wars. [17] As renowned for this spirit of toleration as for their emphasis on reason and conduct, all of which work together to form a harmonious philosophy still Christian, the Latitudinarians abjure "the Anti-christian pride and vanity" of religious dogmatism and exclusivism, arguing instead that "the *Church* consists of all those that agree in the profession, and acknowledgment of the Scripture, and the *first* comprehensive, *plain Creeds*, however scatter'd through the World, and distinguish'd by names of Nations, and Parties, under various degrees of light, and divers models, and forms of Worship, as to circumstance, and order. . . . By which *Catholick* principle, foundation is lay'd for *universal* Charity, and Union." [18]

Considered in the abstract, statements like the last are open to misconstruction. For when the Latitudinarians advocate "*universal* Charity, and Union," just as when they stress the power and place of reason in religious matters, they are more restrictive than the words in themselves suggest. The toleration they earnestly fought for would be limited, and the desired union would be of Protestants, under the leadership of the Church of England, for the purpose of outflanking Catholicism, which they still viewed as a threat to church and state far more dangerous than sectarianism. We must, therefore, put in perspective the laudatory comments of the Latitudinarians' defenders Patrick, Fowler, and Glanvill, themselves "men of Latitude."

Sincere Christians at once devoted to the continuation of the Reformation and "up to date in the ways of the world," [19] the Broad Churchmen were in a very trying position. If religion itself was threatened by an increasingly secular and materialistic society, the Church of England was assailed also by Catholicism and sectarianism. To preserve the hegemony of the Established Church and combat the forces of irreligion, however they might be defined, the Latitudinarians accepted the support offered by the Newtonian world view. If ultimately the means employed spelled destruction of "the clerical world," [20] it was a result opposite from that intended.

As Margaret C. Jacob has argued, the Latitudinarians, some of whom were scientists and all of whom were enamored of science, "used the new mechanical philosophy, that is, their vision of the natural world, to support a political world where private interest would enhance the stability of the public weal and Anglican hegemony would rest secure." [21] In brief, Latitudinarian thinking, itself self-interested, went like this: "If nature could appear to operate according to certain mechanical principles directly controlled by a providential deity and discernible to man, then human desires for power and the acquisition of fortune could be allowed free expression. Nature would provide a model for Christianizing and harmonizing the operations of the 'world politick,' and the church, a comprehensive body of true Protestants, would apply that model and, in the workings of economic and social forces, reveal the operations of providence."[22] Newtonian science, therefore, making possible a sound Christian interpretation of the second book of Scripture just at the moment when the first lost its credibility, provided the Latitudinarians with a means "to control and harness change in such a way that it would serve and preserve their interests."[23]

Believing that the market society had already arrived, the Latitudinarians, many of whom came from trade and commercial backgrounds, taught a natural religion that rested self-interest, which they condoned and fostered,[24] on the Providential order declared in the political and natural worlds. William Derham, promulgator of the extremely popular "physico-theology," makes clear the practical use of the argument from design when he writes: "Thus the wise Governour of the World, hath taken Care for the Dispatch of Business. But then as too long Engagement about worldly Matters would take off Mens Minds from God and Divine Matters, so by this Reservation of every Seventh Day, that great Inconvenience is prevented also."[25] At least implicit in Derham's representative remarks is a view of religion's function quite distinct from that which prevailed prior to the Latitudinarians. That religion "now exists in order to ensure the smooth running of the well-ordered society" is even clearer in Richard Bentley's question to a Hobbesian opponent: "Why, then, dost thou endeavour to undermine this foundation, to undo this *cement of society,* and to reduce all once again to thy imaginary state of nature and original confusion? No community ever was or can be maintained, but upon the basis of religion."[26]

In the Latitudinarians the social function of religion comes perilously close to replacing the spiritual. Church teachings they now directed "toward the public sphere of human activity and away from the private matters of individual piety and worship of the creator."[27] Bentley exhibits this new orientation when he declares at the beginning of his contribution to the Boyle Lectures, themselves a powerful testimony to the marriage of science, society, and religion, "Religion itself gives us the greatest delights and advantages even in this life also, though there should prove in the event to be no resurrection to another. *Her ways are ways of pleasantness and all her paths are peace.*"[28]

Indeed, peacefulness and pleasantness become defining characteristics of Latitudinarianism. In part this preaching of peace and union is directed toward securing a united Protestant front against the revived Catholic threat, Gilbert Burnet going so far as to declare that these, "the main Support of every State . . . must be purchased at any rate."[29] This aim itself derives from the fundamental desire to maintain social order and stability, to preserve the status quo, the guarantor of Anglican hegemony. Rather than buck economic individualism and the market society, the Latitudinarians chose to enlighten self-interest, the motivating force behind the rapidly growing movement. Preserving religion in this context, they reasoned, required accommodation, rather than direct opposition. Thus in a characteristic sermon on "The Advantage of Religion to Societies," Tillotson claims that "there cannot be a greater prejudice raised against any thing than to have it represented as inconvenient and hurtful to our temporal interests."[30] In sermon after sermon, in fact, including such well-known ones as "The Advantages of Religion to Particular Persons," "The Precepts of Christianity Not Grievous," and "Of the Eternity of Hell Torments," Tillotson makes a concerted effort to extenuate the difficulties of the Christian religion, dulcifying its demands. "I shall endeavour to vindicate the reasonableness of this precept of self-denial and suffering for Christ," he says, "which, at first appearance, may seem to be so very harsh and difficult." Wherever the Gospel exacts rigorous demands, we can be sure that "we shall be infinitely gainers by our obedience to them. If we deny our selves any thing in this world for Christ and his Religion, we shall, in the next, be considered for it to the utmost." Appealing more to self-interest than to conscience and the need to correct vices, Tillotson ends by claiming that self-denial "is, in truth and reality, but a more commendable sort of self-love, because we do herein most effectually consult, and secure, and advance our own happiness."[31]

If peace and stability are the ends, pleasantness is the means. Tillotson and Burnet, especially, devote much effort to attacking the "peevishness," bad temper, and ill humor that they claim to see in various threatening attempts to validate doctrinal differences and to make Christianity rigorous and severe. Sometimes it seems that their aim is to reduce opposition to their "moderate" position to just these states of mind. Burnet, who insists that charity takes precedence over faith and hope, holds that "the more strict we are, we become the more hot and peevish." His conclusion, not altogether surprisingly, is that "All our evils flow from our own ill humours."[32] Thus whereas Dryden, who is also interested in "*Common quiet*," insists that pride be curbed and self-assertiveness be restrained, Burnet locates the problem quite differently—and simply—in ill humor.

In the final analysis, Latitudinarianism is best viewed not in isolation, as is the usual scholarly procedure, but in relation to the less prominent but nonetheless important High Church position, which has been slighted in recent scholarship and with which Dryden, interestingly, was often in agreement in the early and mid-1680s. For purposes of comparison I have selected perhaps the most vocal of the High Churchmen in the late seventeenth century, George Hickes, who became Dean of Worcester in 1683 and whom Dryden praised as "that truly Christian author" for his reply to the Whiggish divine Samuel Johnson's *Julian the Apostate*.[33] In that reply, entitled *Jovian* and published in 1683, Hickes scored such clergymen for reasons similar to those that soon aroused his vigorous opposition to the Latitudinarians. A religious and political conservative who clung to Divine Right and passive obedience while insisting on the rigorous, demanding, and severe nature of Christian faith, Hickes claimed that his opponents had "indeed most accurately painted the *Jailes*, and *Fetters*, and *Dungeons*, and *Gibbets*, and *Flames*, and all other Instruments of Torment to provoke them beyond the Measures of Christian Patience, but they have said nothing of *Faith, Hope,* and *the Love of God,* and of the *Special Assistances* which he gives in times of Persecution, because the Considera- tion of these Things would at the same time have spoiled their Design by quieting the Minds of their Readers, and qualifying their Fears, and letting them see that Persecution really was not so Terrible, and Intolerable, as they presented it to be."[34] By no means favoring the succession of a Catholic—he wrote in 1674 that "I am as sorry as any other man, that [Exclusion] was not alwaies one of the Fundamental Laws of *England,* though now it be too late to make it such"[35]—Hickes nevertheless taught that even persecution was preferable to violating God's will repre- sented in the laws of the state and embodied in the traditional Anglican doctrine of passive obedience. Indeed, he argues in *Jo- vian,* persecution and the threat of persecution test the mettle of a Christian and provide wonderful opportunities to live the life of faith, which he interprets differently from the Latitudinar- ians. The duties of the Christian are thus clear; as he expressed the point in *The True Nature of Persecution Stated,* a sermon deliv- ered in 1681, "Christianity is a suffering Religion, and above all others exposeth its Professors to Persecution, because when the Supreme Power happens to be Infidel, Idolater or Heretick, and so sets it self against the Gospel in general, or any particular Truth of it, it becomes the Duty of all Christian subjects to suffer if they will not fly. There's no mean in the Gospel betwixt these two Extremes, denying the Faith or fighting in the Defence of it, being equally damning Sins."[36]

Remaining true to his principles, Hickes, after the revolu- tion, refused to swear allegiance to William and Mary, whom he regarded as usurpers of the throne rightly, if unfortunately, be- longing to James. During this period much of his time was spent in attacking the Latitudinarians for what he saw as violations of Anglican principle and of the very nature of the Christian religion. For not only did such men as Tillotson, Stillingfleet, and Burnet forswear passive obedience and pledge support of the "usurpers," but they and the church seemed to grow fat as a result of this "unholy compromise." Hickes's point is per- fectly clear when he praises those who "prefer the Truth and

Honour of their Religion, before the Lands and Revenues of the Church."[37]

In various works he lashes the Latitude-men for undercutting the church's spiritual function through involvement in the secular and political and, in fact, insuring her utter dependence on the state. In *Two Treatises, One of the Christian Priesthood, The Other of the Dignity of the Episcopal Order,* Hickes insists on the independent nature of the church and on its distinction as a society from the state; in his view, like Dryden's, church and state should be "subordinate, and subject to one another; the Church to the State in all temporal Matters, and the State to the Church in purely spiritual Matters."[38]

Focusing on "that *Latitude,* which hath corrupted Divinity to such a deplorable degree, and set Men free from almost all the Doctrines of Christianity, and all the Principles which relate to the Church, as a *Society,* or as a *Sect,*" Hickes maintains that this "Latitude of Opinion is one of the Reasons, why so many Ministers of late are more than ever *secularized* in their Conversation, and without Reverence to themselves, conform themselves, and Families, to the Sinful Fashions, and Vanities of the World, against which they ought to preach with one Mouth." Holding a high estimation of the clergy's duties as exemplars of the faith they profess, he writes, "Clergymen so often value themselves more upon some other Character, or Account, than as the Ministers of God, and by their own Example teach the Laity to do so too."[39]

In Hickes's dogged insistence on the individual Christian's obligation to suffer rather than fight even civil persecution appears the theme of self-denial that figures so prominently in sermon after sermon devoted to nonpolitical topics. A staunch traditionalist, Hickes defines religion as "nothing but a body of commanding, and prohibiting laws, enacted by God, for his creatures to observe."[40] Though he recognizes and teaches the necessity of embodying faith in good works, the premium in his writings is more on obedience to God's laws than the practice of particular virtues. Difficult in themselves, those laws are even harder to observe due to the lures of the temporal and carnal.

Refusing to minimize the difficulties the Christian believer must face and overcome if he is to follow God's wishes, Hickes unashamedly, indeed proudly, teaches that the path is straight and narrow. He readily admits that the temptations, internal and external, are so great that many will swerve and falter.

> The Doctrine of *Saving Justifying Faith* is a very severe Doctrine, which involves a far greater part of Christians in the dreadful State of Damnation, than I am willing to name. The same I may say of the Doctrines of *Continence, Temperance,* and *Sobriety,* and *Chastity;* of *Truth, Justice,* and *Common Honesty* in our Words and Actions; especially of the Rigid Doctrine concerning Promises and asserting Oaths, all which at some time or other, as the World will plead, are grievous to be born. I may say the same of any Doctrine of Faith, the Belief of which is necessary to Salvation; for Example, that of our Saviour's being God and Man in one Person, and of the same Substance with the Father as he is God.[41]

Shortly thereafter he adds, making explicit what has been at least implicit all along, "I cannot make the Gate wider, nor the way easier or broader, than Christ hath made it. I can make no new Gospel for any Number of Men, tho' never so great; and if Numbers of Men of *Latitudinarian* Principles and Practices will involve themselves in the Consequences of Christian Truths, it is they and they only who make them conclude severely upon themselves."[42]

Hickes's intense Augustinianism and thus his fierce hatred of Latitudinarianism may be summarized with reference to his most direct assault on Latitudinarian principles and practices, which occurs in the abusive *Some Discourses upon Dr. Burnet and Dr. Tillotson; Occasioned by the Late Funeral Sermon of the Former upon the Later* (1695). "It was my Design in writing these Discourses," Hickes declares in the preface, "to aim at all the Men of this *broad Way*" of thinking. He thus reprobates Tillotson for having supported William of Orange, insinuates an earlier involvement of Tillotson with the Whigs and the Duke of Monmouth, and claims that the Archbishop's actions against the nonjurors perfectly reflect the man: "this Spirit of Persecution in him proceeds from a Spirit of *Latitude*, which makes him he cannot endure the Men of strict suffering Principles."[43]

At the center of Hickes's hatred of Tillotson lies his opposition to the new interpretation of Christian demands and requirements, offered by Tillotson, Burnet, and others. He spends some time, therefore, on "another Blemish of his life," Tillotson's famous sermon in which "he openly and directly writes against the Eternity of Hell Torments." Typically opposing any dulcification of the rigors of the Christian faith, Hickes affirms the reality of hell torments, "which God hath not only threatened as a Judge, and solemnly enacted and decreed as a Lawgiver, but our Saviour taught, as the great Doctor and Prophet of his Church." Tillotson, though, had suggested the possibility of repentance in the next world. This, asserts Hickes, was "a most presumptuous, dangerous, and heretical Insinuation": "And accordingly when it was first Published, the Atheists, and Deists, and Socinians of the Town, carried it about them to show it in all Places, glorying everywhere in the Doctrines of it, and extolling the Author for a Man who durst speak Truth, and set Mankind free from the Slavish Notion of eternal Torments."[44] As a reading of Tillotson's sermon makes clear, hardly anything could be further from his intention. Nevertheless, as Hickes claimed, the Deists and others seized upon the sermon's unmistakable dulcifying aspect, Anthony Collins exclaiming, "What a charming Idea does he give us of the *Deity*."[45]

Tillotson's uneasy position in the sermon "Of the Eternity of Hell Torments" is emblematic of Latitudinarianism generally. While never denying that eternal punishment is a real possibility, Tillotson stresses that God is not obliged to execute what he has threatened; he "sees the doctrine as a general deterrent rather than a judicial response to particular offenses."[46] Though small, the crack in the wall of orthodoxy is just large enough to comfort the free-thinkers and to anger the traditionalists, both of whom realized the unintended implications of the new position. Other Latitudinarian arguments were similarly put to uses the churchmen sincerely reprobated. They were from the first opposed by stricter interpreters, who, perhaps more judicious, better understood the eventual consequences of any mitigation, extenuation, or accommodation of Christian doctrine.

The evidence I have adduced suggests that Harth and Budick err when they identify Dryden's position in the early 1680s with Latitudinarianism. For a while, as I have suggested, his thinking did resemble that of Tillotson, Burnet, Stillingfleet, and other "moderate" Anglicans; certainly his allegiance to the new science and the accompanying sanguine hopes for commercial progress, as well as a general enlightened spirit that produced antiauthoritarianism and opposition to superstition and more positively an irenicism and an intellectual and economic individualism, recall the inclinations of the Latitude-men. Though it may not have required it, Dryden's rejection of these ideas and of the market society and its bourgeois values in the late 1670s signals a turn from something like Latitudinarian thinking to a position in many respects closer to that of Hickes and other High Churchmen. Dryden cannot, of course, be identified with the High Churchmen precisely on account of his fierce anticlericalism. As a matter of fact, the High Churchmen reacted even more violently than the Latitudinarians to charges of priestcraft, Hickes smiting those who "blasphemously call the *divine Institution* of Priesthood, by the spiteful name of *Priestcraft*" and who contend, like Dryden, whose phrasing he contemptuously echoes, that "*all Religions, and Priests of all Religions are the same.*" [47]

Since the points of divergence between Dryden and the Latitudinarians are implicit in the foregoing discussions, we need now only summarize them briefly. Dryden's view of religion by the 1680s approximated Robert South's, who wrote that "it is only a pious life, led *exactly* by the rules of a *severe* religion, that can authorize a man's conscience to speak comfortably to him." [48] In *Religio Laici* Dryden pointedly defines the Christian religion in terms of its opposition to self-interest and so clearly distinguishes himself from those who argue that religion "condones and fosters the pursuit of self-interest":[49]

> This *onely* Doctrine does our *Lusts* oppose:
> Unfed by Natures Soil, in which it grows;
> Cross to our *Interests*, curbing Sense, and Sin.
>
> (ll. 158–60)

Whether or not Dryden aimed these lines at the Latitudinarians, his strong opposition in this poem to the Deist's "*easie God* [who] instructs Thee to *rebell*" (l. 96) and in *The Medall* to Shaftesbury's "jolly God, that passes hours too well / To promise Heav'n, or threaten us with Hell" (ll. 279–80) betokens a conception of the Deity at some remove from the Latitudinarians', who, though less blatantly than their opponents claimed, dulcified his actions toward man, including the controverted possibility of eternal punishment.

In any case, well before the conversion Dryden explicitly attacked Latitudinarians, including Samuel Johnson and Gilbert Burnet in *The Second Part of Absalom and Achitophel*. Thinking principally of the Cambridge Platonists, Earl Miner claims that the Latitudinarians are in fact the first party attacked in *Religio Laici*, this occurring in the Preface when Dryden rebukes "our Modern Philosophers, nay and some of our Philosophising Divines [who] have too much exalted the faculties of our Souls." Moreover, Dryden's satirical references to the materialism of the Anglican clergy in the poems of the early 1680s can only be aimed at the Latitudinarians. Finally, their apparent slighting of the clergy's spiritual function in favor of a pragmatically induced focus on matters secular and even political does more than run counter to Dryden's unwavering call for clerical purity from *The Indian Emperour* through "The Character of a Good Parson"; it also forms an important context for viewing his attempt, beginning with *Mac Flecknoe*, to perform certain necessary priestly functions currently being neglected by churchmen. Latitudinarian failure, we may say, provides at least part of the motivation

for his most famous poems, including *Religio Laici;*[50] betraying
their function and their Christ, at least some Latitudinarians
had, in Dryden's view, become priests of Mammon serving the
world.

Dryden's emphasis on Latitudinarians following his conversion to Catholicism, and especially after the revolution, is
much more than the reflection of differences between churches.
It reflects the important consistency in his opposition to churchmen, for by their actions in the late 1680s and 1690s the Latitudinarians confirmed his blackest suspicions and, at least in
his own eyes, justified his long-standing sense that priests,
typically greedy and self-interested, would, when given the
chance, "Viper-like, devour" that which they were sworn to
serve and support. With a parallel that he found fascinating if
lamentable, the Latitudinarians seemed to earn the censure that
he had earlier given the Puritans:

> Religions name against it self was made;
> The shadow serv'd the substance to invade:
> Like Zealous Missions they did care pretend
> Of souls in shew, but made the Gold their end.
> (*Astraea Redux*, ll. 191–94)

The clerical leadership of the Church of England was, then,
moving in a direction opposite from Dryden's. Whereas he had
recently but decisively turned toward "the old order" for his
values and ground, the emergent Latitudinarians, seemingly
caught between two worlds neither of which they could whole-
heartedly embrace, chose to graft Christian thinking onto the
mechanical but serviceable Newtonian world view and to accommodate their religion to the needs of a market society while
enlightening its self-interest in order to preserve the church.
Their emphases were decidedly modernistic, the transforma-
tions of traditional teaching they effected of considerable magni-
tude. To a man in the late seventeenth century equipped like
Dryden or Hickes with a sensibility attuned to traditional val-

ues, the Latitudinarians, despite crucial differences readily apparent at this distance, might well appear very close to Deists and free-thinkers.

Helping to determine the direction of Anglicanism at this time, and so contributing not a little to Dryden's disenchantment with the Established Church, was its "serious crisis of authority,"[51] ignited by Martin Clifford's *Treatise of Humane Reason*, which generated at least ten responses between its publication in 1674 and the mid-1680s. Whether or not Dryden consciously addressed his layman's faith as in part a reply to this important tract by his longtime foe, the *Treatise's* extreme emphasis on the power of the private reason and its ultimate internalization of authority run directly counter to Dryden's attempt in that poem to "*guide* us upward." What we must consider now is the nature and full extent of the crisis generated by Clifford and its implications for Dryden's relation to Anglicanism.

The ostensible occasion of Clifford's book, like that of Dryden's *Religio Laici*, concerns specifics of scriptural interpretation. Professing to accept the Bible as God's revelation to mankind, Clifford claims that with the Reformation every individual was granted the right to interpret the Scriptures for himself. Rejecting the private spirit, as well as General Councils and church tradition, he maintains that only the private reason or private conscience, as he calls it, is of use in understanding the Bible. His divergence from accepted Anglican doctrine appears in the fact that "setting aside the traditional Anglican limitation of private reason to the discovery of plain truths necessary to salvation, he insists that the principle of private conscience, proclaimed by the reformers, extends to the more obscure passages of Scripture as well."[52]

In the course of the ensuing controversy the original issue of private interpretation of matters essential to salvation and submission to the church's pronouncements on things indifferent became blurred and eventually transformed into "a simple choice between private judgment and ecclesiastical authority, with Clifford's opponents defending the latter."[53] As a result two principal and telling arguments emerged to challenge the teaching authority of the Established Church. One of these was Albertus Warren's contention that a church which disclaims infallibility cannot logically compel submission to her interpretation of Scripture or impose beliefs upon her followers. The other, more important, argument was expressed by both Clifford and his patron George Villiers, Duke of Buckingham, who, like Clifford, contributed to *The Rehearsal* and whom Dryden depicted as Zimri in *Absalom and Achitophel.* This is the argument that the logical outcome of the Reformation, which they professed a desire to complete, "is the rejection of all church authority and the pursuit of private reason to wherever it may lead the individual [layman.]"[54] In Buckingham's terms:

When the Reformers had cast off the unsufferable Bondage of *Rome,* and rescu'd the Gospel from the Impositions and Impostures of that Church, one wou'd have imagin'd they should have cast away that odious Maxim of confining and imposing on the Consciences of those, they had set free; and never have dreamt of Persecuting them for making use of that Liberty, they had pretended to establish, by requiring an implicit Faith in them, and their Doctrines, when they wou'd not allow it to those of the Church, they had forsaken for her Errors, and Tyranny. For to me it is very unaccountable, that they should pretend to tell us, that we should now freely consult the Word of God, and at the same time deny us to understand it for our selves; since that is but to Fool us with the name of Liberty, without letting us possess the thing, and we might as well have continu'd under our old Masters, as be Slaves to new Lords. And this I believe has stopt the Progress of the Reformation.[55]

Somewhat like Milton, whose similar hopes had been blasted when the events of the 1640s proved that "new presbyter is but old priest writ large," and like Dryden, who claimed that "Priests of all Religions are the same," Warren lamented, in a representative statement, "the general Disease of Ecclesiasticks every where."[56] Thus the conclusion, of at least Clifford and Buckingham, as expressed by the latter: "There is no way, indeed, left to make the *Reformation* flourish, but [the church's] espousing sincerely *a true and perfect Liberty of Conscience; that is, that it make the Empire of Reason sacred, and not to be invaded by any Party.*"[57]

Clifford's opponents presented no satisfactory reply to either of the two positions designed to minimize church authority. That they could offer only assertions, not arguments, reveals the dilemma Clifford, Warren, and Buckingham had created for the Church of England. She was simply "caught in an untenable position between two alternatives, neither of which she could adopt."[58] Generally preferring ecclesiastical authority to the alternative of unbridled private reason, the Anglican apologists in responding to Clifford sometimes verged on the Catholic position.

Though outweighed in numbers in the controversy itself, the Clifford side could, then, lay claim to victory, not only because their arguments went largely unrebutted but also because the dominant party within the Church of England was at that moment deemphasizing the teaching authority of the church in favor of a new stress on charity and conduct. In a number of ways, indeed, the epithet "latitudinarian" fits the "good-natured" and tender-conscienced[59] Clifford, Warren, and Buckingham. Warren believed, for example, that "External Ceremonies" are "but the shell of Religion," and Clifford proudly acknowledged that his doctrine "sets the great gate of Heaven so wide open, that it will displease those men, who with an envious kind of pride think it more honour to enter in with a few at a narrow wicket. But I truly, out of an humble consideration of my own weakness, and the general imbecility of humane nature, should still lament and tremble, that the entrances to Heaven are so few and so difficult, though they were yet far more and much easier than this opinion makes them."[60] Being with only two exceptions High Churchmen,[61] Clifford's opponents seize upon such resemblances in order to link him and his supporters with Latitudinarianism. The most obvious such attempt was by John Warly, who titled his second contribution to the controversy *The Reasoning Apostate: or Modern Latitude-Man Consider'd, as He Opposeth the Authority of the King and Church* (1677).[62] Though clearly latitudinarian, Clifford, Warren, and Buckingham must, of course, be distinguished from those "moderate" Anglican churchmen whom they on occasion singled out for special praise. For the former the Reformation would be completed at the expense of the church, whose clergy as a body they regarded as an impediment to reform and progress.

With at least their attempt to minimize church authority Dryden in the early 1680s would agree. But his differences from Clifford and his defenders are much greater than this important similarity. Not completely taken with the Reformation, Dryden thought that "This good had full as bad a Consequence" (*Religio Laici,* l. 399). Moreover, the century's trend toward internalizing authority, exemplified in Clifford, constituted his focus in his layman's faith, which proposes absolute reliance on authority outside the self. What surely frightened Dryden, causing him perhaps to reconsider his relationship to the Church of England, were the far-reaching implications of Clifford's position. A. M., the author of *Plain-Dealing,* the first response to Clifford, recognized that his opponent's motives in publishing *A Treatise of Humane Reason* were political. Supporting his claim that the main thrust of Clifford's effort is "general Toleration of all Religions"[63] is the fact that the Duke of Buckingham introduced in Parliament a bill to just this effect on 16 November 1675. Clifford, Warren, and Buckingham were, of course, Whigs; Warren dedicated his *Apology for the Discourse of Humane Reason* to Shaftesbury, and Buckingham's politics are too well known to require documentation.

Other consequences, political and theological, of the position taken by Clifford, Warren, and Buckingham are readily apparent. Warren's statement that reason "is antecedent to all Laws, and therefore the Determiner of the Rectitude and Obliquity of every Action,"[64] is radically antiauthoritarian and individualistic. The same holds for Clifford's prized freedom of inquiry, which exceeds the bounds the scientists and Latitudinarians at least claimed to respect. Like Warren, Clifford writes that "no Authority is obeyable or believable in it self without farther examination: no not that of God himself" and that nothing can oblige "us to a blind and inalterable observance of those Laws and Opinions, which either the fate of our birth and education, or the fortune of other accidents have engaged us in; but we ought to make a serious and long enquiry, whether they agree most with that light of our Understanding, which God has infused into us for that end, according to the best extent of those means, which are allowed by him to our understandings for this examination." [65] According to the author of *Plain-Dealing*, Clifford's fundamental principle, whereby "every mans Reason would be his Magistrate, and he should be onely bound to do that which is right in his own eyes," cannot "be allowed to any person that is subject to the Laws of any Society." If the common people rely wholly upon reason, "by thinking themselves as wise as their Teachers, [they will] come to despise and contemn them, and to trample under foot all Order and Decency." [66]

The implications of Clifford's position extend beyond politics and beyond the contention of *Reason Regulated* that the master of the Charterhouse "authoriseth every Particular Person, in Spirituals to be his own Judge, and Pastor." [67] According to Warly, in Clifford reason exalts "*it self above* Sacred Authority . . . *Usurping its power, pleading* [its own] claim and *right to the* Spiritual Judicature." [68] The anonymous author of *The Spirit of Prophecie* makes the point most directly when he declares that Clifford and his followers are guilty of usurping the place of God and of making him their inferior: reason, he writes, "gives them the rule over him, and supposeth them able to attain to happiness whether he will give it them or no, and so (without a Metaphor) to take the Kingdome of Heaven by force, and to commit a Rape upon the Almighty." [69] These same charges Dryden leveled at his opponents in the early 1680s. They in fact reflect his central concerns at the time.

In opposition to Clifford, Warren, and Buckingham, Dryden could have found in the controversy they generated a not-altogether-surprising ally in the anonymous Catholic author of *Reason Regulated*. Though Dryden had much in common with the Anglican participants in the controversy, their inability to defend the historical position of the Church of England as a *via media* between Roman authoritarianism and sectarian individualism seriously compromised for him their attractiveness, as well as that of Anglicanism. Viewed in the context of this weakness, the logic and strong decisiveness of the Catholic arguments could only appear to gain. With no hesitation whatsoever, the Catholic apologist insists on principle that "our business, and duty . . . is to obey, and not dispute." Sharing Dryden's emphasis in *Religio Laici* on God and insufficient man's need to rely on power and authority beyond the self, though arriving at a different conclusion, that author declares that our Blessed Savior "has not left the Condition of Mankind in this endless Confusion, but has miraculously Founded, and Signaliz'd a Church to end all Controversyes." [70] Though Dryden readily agreed that "*God wou'd not leave Mankind without a way*" (*Religio Laici*, 1. 296), he could not in 1682 accept that that way was provided in, by, and through the church, whether Catholic or Anglican. On that crucial point he took the position of the layman's faiths, which was in certain respects congenial with, and even anticipatory of, the Clifford-Warren-Buckingham thinking; interpreting *Scriptura sola* radically, *Religio Laici* attempts an alternative to the latter independent of the church.

How Dryden came to change his mind within a few years and to accept the central Catholic argument that "Apostolical Tradition, not Written Books, *etc.* is . . . the true, and certain Rule of Faith," [71] is the issue at hand. In attempting to confront it, we have first to consider the various attractions Restoration Catholicism held for one of Dryden's sensibility and outlook. Once that is done, we may be better able to understand how he overcame his intense opposition to priestly rule and church authority.

Before we turn directly to the doctrines and practice of Catholicism in the Restoration, it may not be amiss to reconsider briefly Dryden's own response to Catholics in the years just before conversion. Though I treated this matter generally and at least indirectly in Chapter Three, some necessary points have not yet been sufficiently emphasized. In *Absalom and Achitophel,* Dryden tried to approach the idea of a heinous Popish Plot with some balance (see ll. 108–17, quoted in Chapter Three); Dryden extenuated any Jesuit treachery by implying that Catholic priests were no worse than any other, including the Anglican, who similarly "espouse his Cause by whom they eat and drink" (l. 107). *The Spanish Fryar* seems likewise designed to mitigate Catholic involvement in the current political turmoil, Dominic being pointedly relegated to the comic plot where his intrigues are limited to the amorous. In Dryden's opinion, as he put it in the Preface to *Religio Laici,* the Papists were "the less dangerous (at least in appearance to our present State) for not onely the Penal Laws are in Force against them, and their number is contemptible; but also their Peerage and Commons are excluded from Parliaments, and consequently those Laws are in no probability of being Repeal'd." Naturally, he defends, as in *The Vindication of The Duke of Guise,* James's succession. But not all Dryden's comments on Catholics in the late 1670s and early 1680s are directed to their political posture, as *The Spanish Fryar* indicates. Surprisingly, at least in view of the usual, though misleading, attribution of militant anti-Catholic sentiments to Dryden, he more than once expressed pity and sympathy for the plight of Catholics. This emerges through his disgust at Popeburning in the Prologue he contributed to Southerne's *The Loyal Brother* (1682), his condemnation of poets who indulge in such incitement as had surrounded the furor over the "Plot" (the Epilogue to *Oedipus*), and, perhaps most importantly, his compassionate treatment of the Jebusites in *Absalom and Achitophel:*

> Th' inhabitants of old *Jerusalem*
> Were *Jebusites:* the Town so call'd from them;
> And their's the Native right————

But when the chosen people grew more strong,
The rightfull cause at length became the wrong:
And every loss the men of *Jebus* bore,
They still were thought God's enemies the more.
Thus, worn and weaken'd, well or ill content,
Submit they must to *David*'s Government:
Impoverisht, and depriv'd of all Command,
Their Taxes doubled as they lost their Land,
And, what was harder yet to flesh and blood,
Their Gods disgrac'd, and burnt like common wood.

(ll. 85–97)

In the early 1680s, therefore, Dryden did not harbor quite the fear and hatred of Catholicism that we have been led to believe and that has helped to make his conversion appear so enigmatic.

Understanding of that conversion has been impeded not only by confusions surrounding Dryden's own stated response to Catholicism prior to 1685 but also by distortions concerning especially the political nature of Restoration Catholicism, owing mainly to the lingering influence of Whig historians. Only recently, in fact, have scholars begun to clear away the many, often vicious, misconceptions regarding Catholicism in this period. In the forefront of this badly needed effort has been John Miller's *Popery and Politics in England 1660–1688*. His conclusion, based on exhaustive research, deserves emphasis. Miller writes that, comprising only a small fraction of England's population, perhaps as little as 10 percent, the majority of Catholics were not involved in political disputes. If the concerns of the laity were primarily with living a normal Catholic life, the "concerns of the priesthood were primarily spiritual and they saw their mission in that light. . . . Apart from one or two meddlers at court the English Catholic clergy were not involved in any politics other than ecclesiastical controversies." Thus Miller destroys the myth of "the continued militancy of the Catholic church, which in fact had subsided by now into a cautious determination to maintain the *status quo*." [72]

Strongly supporting this interpretation of the Catholic political stance is the evidence supplied by both principle and the testimony of apologists, clerical and lay alike. Of primary concern to Protestants, of course, was the claim, particularly as bruited by the theorists of the Counter-Reformation, that the pope could and would excommunicate princes and declare them deposed, absolving subjects of their political allegiance. Though the seventeenth-century Church officially retained this so-called theory of the deposing power, it took "no steps to put it into practice."[73] Hardly anyone regarded the theory as more than problematical, and at least by the time he wrote *The Vindication of The Duke of Guise* in 1683 Dryden was convinced that the pope would not now employ this deposing power. According to the author of *Reflexions upon the Oathes of Supremacy and Allegiance*, "This pretended article of faith is by such new *de-fide* men grounded either on the actions of certain popes since pope Gregory VII, which both for their own sake and ours it is to be wished had never been done, or might be blotted out of men's memories; or upon the decrees of some councils not received or acknowledged by Catholic churches."[74] While many apologists denied it as an article of faith, others condemned it outright, including E. Cary in *The Catechist Catechiz'd* and W. H. in *English Loyalty Vindicated by the French Divines*, both published in 1681. In 1679, apparently speaking for most of his fellow Catholics, Sir John Winter declared that although they acknowledge "the pope is the supreme spiritual pastor . . . yet the Roman Catholics do not hold it as part of their faith that the pope is infallibly free from error, or that he can absolve subjects from their obedience to their natural prince, or from the obligation of faithful upright dealing with their neighbours, though such their prince or their neighbour be not of their religion, or were excommunicated."[75] Even more direct is the claim of William Blundell: "All Catholic subjects of a lawful Protestant king (such as king Charles the 2nd) are obliged faithfully to adhere to that king in all invasions whatsoever, though made by Catholic princes or even by the pope himself."[76]

Rather than mitigate his sense of allegiance and obligation to the king, the apologist Hugh Paulinus Cressy found that his conversion to Catholicism actually increased his "fidelity to temporall Superiors."[77] The reasons for this are not difficult to discover. "Preeminently a system, a discipline," Catholicism "compels the subordination of individual experience to that of the community."[78] Moreover, according to Dryden in 1681, whereas "no Government but a Commonwealth is accommodated to the Systeme of Church-worship invented by *John Calvin,*" the Catholic Church, simply by preaching obedience, appeared "thoroughly compatible with monarchical authority."[79] In fact, according to *Rushworth's Dialogues,* "our Forms [are well suited] for regulating the Commonwealth," for "nothing makes the people so faithfull and obedient."[80] With some justification, therefore, Sir Henry Capel declared in 1679, "Lay Popery flat, and there's an end of arbitrary government and power; it is a mere chimera or notion without Popery."[81] More moderate, the Marquis of Halifax noted the authoritarianism and opposition to assertive individualism inherent in Catholicism: liberty and infallibility, he maintained, are "the two most contrary things that are in the world. The church of Rome doth not only dislike the allowing liberty, but by its principles it cannot do it."[82] What Roman Catholicism held out to Dryden, then, as Miner has suggested, was in part an "ecclesiastical analogy to his royalism."[83]

As it happens, of course, it is on the issue of the individual's relationship to Scripture, a matter of central importance to Dryden, that Catholic rejection of private authority appears most clearly; here too the poet found an ecclesiastical analogy to his own general principles. Symbolized in the title of one of the important polemics of the late seventeenth century, this issue of scriptural interpretation is for Catholicism *The Question of Questions, which Rightly Resolv'd resolves All our Questions in Religion. The Question is, Who ought to be our Judge in all these Differences?* In accord with Dryden's own views as early as *Religio Laici,* but quite unlike Clifford, Warren, and Buckingham, as well as the Latitudinarians, Catholics contended that "Christ did not bid all common people *search the Scriptures.*"[84] Freedom of interpretation, they argued, inevitably produces dissension, division, and atomism, the author of *Reason Regulated* contending that Clifford's "*Latitudinarian*, or *Socinian* Doctrine, does not onely Untie and Unbind, but Blends, and Shuffles all into a *Chaos*."[85] Bossuet sums up the Catholic position as follows:

> Let a Man make what profession he pleaseth to submit himself to the Word of God, if every one think he has a right to Interpret it according to his own Sense, and against the Tenets of the Church declared in her last Sentence, this Pretension *will open a door to all sorts of Extravagancies; it will take away all the means of supplying a remedy;* because the Decision of the Church is not a Remedy to those, who think themselves not obliged to submit to it; in fine, it gives way to the *framing as many Religions,* not only *as there are Parishes,* but also as there are Persons.[86]

Such claims to religious authority and certainty "appealed most to Charles II, James II and other converts."[87]

Also of major importance to Dryden at least was the nature of the Catholic priesthood in the Restoration. As Miller says, their concerns "were primarily spiritual and they saw their mission in that light." In this regard they differed significantly from the ascendant party in the Established Church, who more and more involved themselves in the secular and even political. Whether or not the purity Dryden had long sought in the Christian clergy was more likely to be found in the Restoration in the Catholic than the Anglican, the attention to the spiritual function he demanded of churchmen seemed more fully to characterize the Catholic.

In addition to reflecting the different emphases in the respective church doctrines, sanctity being the one "mark" of the church omitted in the Anglican version of the Nicene Creed, the actions of the two priesthoods helped shape the conduct of their respective laity. Brandishing traditional concepts whose force the Latitudinarians tended to blunt, Catholic apologists insisted on the spiritual nature of the Christian religion, John Sergeant

tion to the priesthood and church authority. Though this problem must not be minimized, points noted above provide a
context in which at least part of the difficulty dissolves. It is important that for several years prior to the conversion Dryden did
not appear particularly antagonistic toward the Catholic clergy.
In fact, in work after work during the years when his anticlericalism was fiercest, he focused principally on Anglican
churchmen. Moreover, as we have seen, by the time Dryden
wrote *Religio Laici,* his opposition to church authority had begun
to seem less important than the primary need to combat those
forces tending to the overthrow of all external authority. Perhaps bearing most importantly on the conversion was the experience of writing *Religio Laici.* The necessary preparation for that
effort acquainted him with Catholic doctrine and the effective
work of Catholic apologists, particularly as regards the centrality
of scriptural interpretation, but in addition the writing itself of
that poem, and its struggle toward an alternative to private authority that did not require acceptance of the word of churchmen, led before long to his recognition that one must either
grant final religious authority to the individual or concede that
power to the church. Dryden's inability in *Religio Laici* to re-
spond satisfactorily to Father Simon's question concerning the
ambiguity of Scripture on the most fundamental point of all,
Christ's nature, revealed the insubstantiality of his radical interpretation of *Scriptura sola.* That failure loomed even larger when
placed beside the parallel failure of the Anglican apologists in
the Clifford controversy to vindicate the historical position of the
Established Church. Dryden's own experience thus confirmed,
and was in turn confirmed by, what emerged from that controversy: a *via media* seems extremely tenuous and vulnerable. If he
were indeed limited to church authority and the unrestrained
freedom of the private individual for alternatives, Dryden's
choice would not be difficult; it was further simplified by the religious and political direction the Church of England appeared
to be taking. A church thus began to appear not only necessary
but desirable, and such a church had to be authoritative.

As others have suggested,[91] Dryden's reading—especially of the Clifford controversy and Catholic apologetics—must have played an important role in his eventual decision to embrace Roman Catholicism. Particularly if, after reaching the impasse of his layman's faith, he turned back to such apologists as Cressy, mentioned in the Preface to that poem as "Father *Cres*," Dryden found situations mirroring his own and thus assisting the movement urged by other forces. In his account of his own path to the Church of Rome, Cressy, a Benedictine who had converted from Anglicanism and who centers on Chillingworth's well-known thesis that the Bible is the religion of Protestants, relates difficulties similar to Dryden's and expresses the same sense of inner peace the poet later described as enjoying himself. "Had it not been for this point of the Churches Infallibility, and some Philosophical Objections against the Real Presence, &c," Cressy writes, "I had not lived thus long out of the communion of the Roman Church." For a long while, somewhat attracted to the temper and morality of Socinianism, "I could not free my selfe from so much partiality against my owne understanding, as to wish that it could be made appeare unto me, that there were to be found any tribunall whose decisions I might believe my self obliged to follow without any scruple or tergiversation." Eventually, however, Cressy found "a full, effectuall and experimental satisfaction by acknowledging this authority, and suffering my selfe to be taken out of my owne hands, to be conducted by her that Christ has appointed for that office." Cressy presents the issue as moral and theological: whether the individual will humble himself, abase his own power, and submit to One outside the self. So described, this would instantly have attracted Dryden's attention and respect. It is the issue that he centers on in *Religio Laici*, when he attacks self-sufficiency without altogether avoiding individualistic self-assertion himself. With Cressy's help, therefore, he could have recognized in his own effort vestiges of the pride he opposed, the pride in which he implicated himself in the *confessio* in the First Part of *The Hind and the Panther:* "My pride struck out new sparkles of her own" (l. 75). In that later poem submission to the church comes to symbolize the conquest of pride that he had unsuc-

alesce, for the impasse reached in *Religio Laici* to achieve full consciousness, for the readings in controversies and apologetics to take hold, and for the necessary recognitions to come about, time was required. At least three years did in fact elapse between the layman's faith and conversion, not a long period for the resolution of long-standing problems and difficulties. In the comments on religious matters in the intervening works can be glimpsed a growing pessimism, perhaps a hardening of position, and, I think, a surer sense of the inevitability of distortion, dissension, and disturbance with the unrestricted allowance of private interpretation of Scripture. Not to be overlooked in the timing of the decision to convert, and perhaps an additional factor influencing that decision, was not only the succession of James II but also the king's proselytizing efforts. By late 1685 he was personally doing "what he could to encourage converts to come forward."[94] Without implying that Dryden stood to gain financially by converting (as a matter of fact, he appeared increasingly attracted to the otherworldly), I think it is clear that the time was then ripe for just this change of faith.

6

Dryden as Catholic Layman

Dryden's deep commitment to Roman Catholicism is reflected in his various literary efforts on behalf of his new church. These began in July 1686, only a few months after the conversion, with the publication of *A Defence of the Papers written by the Late King of Blessed Memory and Duchess of York Against the Answer made to them*; this tract is a rebuttal of Stillingfleet's hasty reply to papers showing that Charles had become reconciled to the Church of Rome and had died a Catholic, papers which also detail the steps of James's first wife's similar conversion.[1] Important in its own right, the *Defence* was excellent preparation for Dryden's poetic account of his new faith, *The Hind and the Panther*, which appeared in May 1687. The same is true of his apparent work translating the first volume of the *Histoire des révolutions arrivées dans l'Europe en Matière de religion*, by Antoine Varillas; Tonson entered the translation in the *Stationers' Register* on 29 April 1686, but it was never published. After *The Hind and the Panther*, drawn, as that poem indicates, to sanctity and examples of self-denial, Dryden translated Bouhours's *Life of St. Francis Xavier* (1687) and included in the *Examen Poeticum* (1693) one of Xavier's favorite hymns, "*Veni Creator Spiritus*, Translated in Paraphrase," which characteristically beseeches God to "Refine and purge our Earthly Parts" and to help us "Submit the Senses to the Soul" (ll. 20, 23).

In the last years of his life Dryden's interest in religious issues continued undiminished, his enthusiasm for the Church of

Rome unabated. At that time he had a son in the Roman priest-hood, and in 1699, the year before he died, he wrote to a young Protestant kinswoman, Elizabeth Steward: "I can neither take the Oaths, nor forsake my Religion, because I know not what Church to go to, if I leave the Catholique; they are all so divided amongst them selves in matters of faith, necessary to Salvation: & yet all assumeing the name of Protestants. May God be pleasd to open your Eyes, as he has opend mine: Truth is but one; & they who have once heard of it, can plead no Excuse, if they do not embrace it."[2] Moreover, his "Character of a Good Parson," published in the *Fables* in 1700, is a full Catholic statement on the priesthood, with the Parson an ideal churchman. It is to this and other lesser known works which express Dryden's later reli-gious thought that I wish to turn, after first treating *The Hind and the Panther.*

The Hind and the Panther supports my argument that Dry-den's conversion represented both change, however pale com-pared with that which occurred eight to ten years earlier, and continuity, being a culmination of tendencies, principles, and desires present for some time. Continuities with earlier posi-tions, and especially with *Religio Laici*, are readily apparent. With one obvious exception Dryden's opponents remain the same, the end is the same (happiness or, here, "bliss," 1:148: "Good life be now my task," 1:78), and this poem too centers on the locus of external authority. Here that authority is the church as God's instrument on earth. Though in the layman's faith Dry-den argued differently that such authority rests in God alone as he speaks in and through Scripture, it is important to note that he thus disagreed with Catholicism not as to whether private in-terpretation of God's Word was permissible but rather in regard to the narrower question of the locus of the ultimate external au-thority that they both insisted on.

Dryden's understanding is therefore different now, but it ap-pears more an outgrowth or deepening of the thought ex-pressed in *Religio Laici* than a complete reversal or repudiation of that earlier position.³ Supporting this interpretation is Dryden's repeated use in *The Hind and the Panther* of the language, imagery, and themes of *Religio Laici*. Though we might expect a poet to distance himself and his readers as far as possible from a work in which he attacked positions now embraced and in which he espoused positions now rejected, it seems clear that Dryden designed the later work to recall its predecessor and to suggest the similarity with difference in the two poems. Leaving aside for the moment the similar thematic concerns which inevitably recall the previous position, among the direct linguistic evocations of *Religio Laici* are such lines as "But how can finite grasp infinity?" (1:105) and "All wou'd be happy at the cheapest rate" (1:375), which echo lines 40 and 397, respectively. More important, the verse paragraph containing the first *confessio* not only reminds us of the content of Dryden's earlier thought, but it also concludes with the same striking imagery with which he began his layman's faith:

> Then let the moon usurp the rule of day,
> And winking tapers shew the sun his way;
> For what my senses can themselves perceive
> I need no revelation to believe.
>
> (1:89–92)

In like manner the imagery at 1:501 ff. recalls the earlier poem:

> Then, as the Moon who first receives the light
> By which she makes our nether regions bright,
> So might she shine, reflecting from afar
> The rays she borrow'd from a better star:
> Big with the beams which from her mother flow
> And reigning o'er the rising tides below.⁴

Dryden evidently wishes us to regard *Religio Laici* as a partial truth, a step in the right direction, a perhaps necessary stage in the development that has at last brought him peace and serenity. Perhaps the later position can be rightly understood only against the background of the earlier thinking.

Thematically this continuity amidst change appears in several different respects. One of the most important has to do with the interpretation of Scripture, the focus of the earlier layman's faith. Dryden's basic fear in *The Hind and the Panther* is, in fact, identical with that five years before: "What weight of antient witness can prevail / If private reason hold the publick scale?" (1:62–63). Here too he approaches the matter of authority through the problem of scriptural interpretation, most fully discussed in the Second Part, which, as Dryden observed in the Preface, "chiefly concern[s] Church Authority." Early on in this part, after noting four theories of infallibility advanced by Catholics, the Hind counsels her Anglican disputant to

> . . . mark how sandy is your own pretence,
> Who setting Councils, Pope, and Church aside,
> Are ev'ry man his own presuming guide.
> The sacred books, you say, are full and plain,
> And ev'ry needfull point of truth contain:
> All who can read, Interpreters may be:
> Thus though your sev'ral churches disagree,
> Yet ev'ry Saint has to himself alone
> The secret of this Philosophick stone.
> (ll. 105–13)

After the Panther objects that she contends "The Word in needfull points is onely plain" (l. 144), the Hind returns to the attack, employing the argument used by Father Simon in *Religio Laici* (ll. 305–15), which Dryden even then had difficulty answering; his opposition to private interpretation in 1682, however, was no less determined than here. To the Panther's demurrer regarding points essential for salvation, the Hind replies:

> Needless or needfull I not now contend,
> For still you have a loop-hole for a friend,

(Rejoyn'd the Matron) but the rule you lay ⎫
Has led whole flocks, and leads them still astray ⎬
In weighty points, and full damnation's way. ⎭
For did not *Arius* first, *Socinus* now,
The Son's eternal god-head disavow,
And did not these by Gospel Texts alone
Condemn our doctrine, and maintain their own?
Have not all hereticks the same pretence
To plead the Scriptures in their own defence?
How did the *Nicene* council then decide
That strong debate, was it by Scripture try'd?
No, sure to those the Rebel would not yield,
Squadrons of Texts he marshal'd in the field;
That was but civil war, an equal set,
When Piles with piles, and eagles Eagles met.
With Texts point-blank and plain he fac'd the Foe:
And did not *Sathan* tempt our Saviour so?

(ll. 145–63)

To the Hind's major point that "The good old Bishops" "by traditions force upheld the truth" (ll. 164, 167), the Panther replies that, though "tradition [may be] join'd with holy writ" (l. 174), the latter remains the rule by which the former must be tried. The Hind's response, asserting Anglican inconsistency, reflects Dryden's concerns throughout the early and mid-1680s and specifically echoes *The Medall*, l. 166:

. . . The Council steer'd it seems a diff'rent course,
They try'd the Scripture by tradition's force;
But you tradition by the Scripture try; ⎫
Pursu'd, by Sects, from this to that you fly, ⎬
Nor dare on one foundation to rely. ⎭
The word is then depos'd, and in this view,
You rule the Scripture, not the Scripture you.
. . . .
. . . when you said tradition must be try'd

By Sacred Writ, whose sense your selves decide,
You said no more, but that your selves must be
The judges of the Scripture sense, not we.
Against our church tradition you declare
And yet your Clerks wou'd sit in *Moyses* chair:
At least 'tis prov'd against your argument,
The rule is far from plain, where all dissent.
(ll. 181–87, 204–11)

Convinced that "amongst equals lies no last appeal" (2:472) and that "no disobedience can ensue, / Where no submission to a Judge is due" (1:485–86)—these passages invoke *Religio Laici*, ll. 93–98—Dryden now grants to the Catholic Church the ultimate authority he had long been seeking. Indeed, adopting in practice "a very distinctive line of radical English Catholicism, which held that tradition alone in the authority of the Church constituted the rule of faith,"[5] Dryden reverses the relative positions of the Bible and of church tradition and authority given in his layman's faith. Just as earlier he minimized the role and power of the church in favor of *Scriptura sola*, so now he elevates the church at the expense of Scripture.

Thus, with due rev'rence, to th' Apostles writ,
By which my sons are taught, to which, submit;
I think, those truths their sacred works contain,
The church alone can certainly explain,
That following ages, leaning on the past,
May rest upon the Primitive at last.
Nor wou'd I thence the word no rule infer,
But none without the church interpreter.
Because, as I have urg'd before, 'tis mute,
And is it self the subject of dispute.
But what th' Apostles their successours taught,
They to the next, from them to us is brought,
Th' undoubted sense which is in scripture sought.

From hence the church is arm'd, when errours rise, ⎫
To stop their entrance, and prevent surprise; ⎬
And safe entrench'd within, her foes without defies. ⎭
By these all festring sores her councils heal, ⎫
Which time or has disclos'd, or shall reveal, ⎬
For discord cannot end without a last appeal. ⎭

(2:351–69)

Earl Miner's observation on this passage is astute:

> It has taken Dryden half of Part II to get as far as admitting
> that the Bible, though itself "no rule," may be one when
> interpreted by the Church. This is no great concession, es-
> pecially in the context of argument after argument for tra-
> dition written and tradition oral; and it is even less of a
> concession because it is followed in less than fifty lines (II,
> 394–400) by the Hind's self-revelation in words like those
> in which "our Saviour own'd his Deity." Claims of this
> kind for the Roman Catholic church are not likely to be
> thought moderate by Protestants, nor does a single con-
> cession, "with due rev'rence, to th' Apostles writ". . .
> seem much more temperate.[6]

Dryden had very nearly finished the journey he began in the
late 1670s.

In developing here the issue of scriptural interpretation and
other recurring themes, Dryden probes somewhat more deeply
than before, seeking to explain both the motivation and the success of his opponents and achieving, I think, an impressive poetic unity; in so doing he reinforces connections between his
Catholic and earlier thinking. Because the "private judgment"
allows for and indeed promotes self-interest, he maintains, it is
bound to attract followers:

. . . they, who left the Scripture to the crowd, ⎫
Each for his own peculiar judge allow'd; ⎬
The way to please 'em was to make 'em proud. ⎭

> Thus, with full sails, they ran upon the shelf;
> Who cou'd suspect a couzenage from himself?
> (2:254–58)

Some lines later, echoing the passage in *Religio Laici* describing the effects of the Reformation,

> Then, every man who saw the Title fair,
> Claim'd a Child's part, and put in for a Share:
> Consulted Soberly his private good;
> And sav'd himself as cheap as e'er he cou'd
> (ll. 394–97)

he specifies the role of "interest" in private interpretation of Scripture, which mediates the texts and imposes on the meaning of God's Word, manipulating passages for its own ends:

> The will is prov'd, is open'd, and is read;
> The doubtfull heirs their diff'ring titles plead:
> All vouch the words their int'rest to maintain,
> And each pretends by those his cause is plain.
> (2:377–80)

Thus "Rul'd by the Scripture and his own advice / Each has a blind by-path to Paradise" (2:124–25). Elsewhere in *The Hind and the Panther* Dryden focuses even more sharply on the determining power of "interest," writing, for example, of its effect on interpretation as well as other intellectual efforts. Though "The *Priest* continues what the nurse began, / And thus the child imposes on the man," "int'rest is the most prevailing cheat":

> They study that, and think they study truth:
> When int'rest fortifies an argument ⎫
> Weak reason serves to gain the wills assent; ⎬
> For souls already warp'd receive an easie bent. ⎭
> (3:391–92, 394, 396–99)

Indeed, in Dryden's depiction of the conflicting faiths, interest is a primary factor distinguishing Catholicism from Protestantism. The origin of Protestantism, he asserts, is deeply mired in "interest," "The jolly *Luther*" [7] having found an "easier" way than that demanded by Catholicism:

> Though our lean faith these rigid laws has giv'n,
> The full fed *Musulman* goes fat to heav'n;
> For his *Arabian* Prophet with delights
> Of sense, allur'd his eastern Proselytes.
> The jolly *Luther*, reading him, began
> T' interpret Scriptures by his *Alcoran;*
> To grub the thorns beneath our tender feet,
> And make the paths of *Paradise* more sweet:
> Bethought him of a wife e'er half way gone,
> (For 'twas uneasy travailing alone;)
> And in this masquerade of mirth and love,
> Mistook the bliss of heav'n for *Bacchanals* above.
>
> (1:376–87)

The Reformation, about which Dryden had long had serious misgivings, he now presents unequivocally as ushering in not only dangerous private interpretation of Scripture but also all manner of religious dissolution, including gratification of the senses at the soul's expense and the triumph of man's fallen inclinations:

> The fruit proclaims the plant; a lawless Prince ⎫
> By luxury reform'd incontinence,   ⎬
> By ruins, charity; by riots, abstinence.   ⎭
> Confessions, fasts and penance set aside;   ⎫
> Oh with what ease we follow such a guide!   ⎬
> Where souls are starv'd, and senses gratify'd.⎭
> Where marr'age pleasures, midnight pray'r supply, ⎫
> And mattin bells (a melancholy cry)   ⎬
> Are tun'd to merrier notes, *encrease* and *multiply.* ⎭

Religion shows a Rosie colour'd face;
Not hatter'd out with drudging works of grace;
A down-hill Reformation rolls apace.
What flesh and bloud wou'd croud the narrow gate,
Or, till they waste their pamper'd paunches, wait?
All wou'd be happy at the cheapest rate.

(1:361–75)

With the opening line of the poem ("A Milk white *Hind*, immortal and unchang'd") Dryden signals his intention to characterize his new church in terms of certain qualities lacking in or subverted by her Protestant opponents, particularly Anglicans. He carefully establishes a series of nearly interlocking contrasts: Catholic faith versus Anglican reason and sense ("God thus asserted: man is to believe / Beyond what sense and reason can conceive," 1:118–19); faithful adherence to principle versus incertitude ("Her wild belief on ev'ry wave is tost," 1:430); self-denial versus compromise (transubstantiation exposes the celebrated Anglican *via media:* "The lit'ral sense is hard to flesh and blood," 1:428, and "To take up half on trust, and half to try, / Name it not faith, but bungling biggottry," 1:141–42); thus the unity, purity, and constancy of the Hind (e.g., 2:526–32) versus the unholy mixture and inconstancy in the Panther: "fairest creature of the spotted kind" (1:328), in whom "faults and vertues lye so mix'd" (1:333), she possesses a "wandring heart" (1:338). Fundamental to her myriad faults, Dryden says, is self-interest, opposition to which he made a defining characteristic of Christianity as early as *Religio Laici.* Even such virtues as her support of the monarchy reflect self-concern: "Nor will I meanly tax her constancy, / That int'rest or obligement made the tye" (1:436–37). In direct contrast with Catholicism, a suffering faith (1:9–24), interest is ingrained in Anglicanism and reflects the Panther's deepest flaws: "Thus fear and int'rest will prevail with some, / For all have not the gift of martyrdome" (2:58–59). The end of the Second Part fittingly and dramatically highlights this contrast, as the Hind graciously welcomes her opponent to her lowly cottage and its "plain fare" (l. 675) and urges her to "pomp disdain, / And dare not to debase your soul to gain" (ll.

712–13). The narrator's following remarks are direct and sharp as they virtually equate Anglicanism with the materialistic interest Dryden had long attacked in the Established clergy:

> The silent stranger stood amaz'd to see
> Contempt of wealth, and wilfull poverty:
> And, though ill habits are not soon controll'd,
> A while suspended her desire of gold.
>
> (ll. 714–17)

There can be no doubt, then, about the continuing attractiveness of the Anglican position. "Be judge your self," says the Hind,

>   if int'rest may prevail,
> Which motives, yours or mine, will turn the scale.
> While pride and pomp allure, and plenteous ease, ⎫
> That is, till man's predominant passions cease, ⎬
> Admire no longer at my slow encrease.[8]   ⎭
>
> (3:384–88)

Even if the Church of England was founded on interest, which it thereafter served ("Immortal pow'rs the term of conscience know, / But int'rest is her name with men below," 3:823–24), recent years, according to Dryden, have seen Christian doctrine more and more perverted and subverted. The Fable of the Doves and Pigeons, recounted by the Hind in the Third Part, testifies impressively to Dryden's own sense of the destruction of the Christian life by "interested" Anglicans,[9] a passage which acquires added importance from its close echo of 1:359–75. At the beginning of this long section appears the contrasting picture of Catholic worship, traditional, disciplined, and rigorous, which sits in severe judgment on the "ease" characteristic of recent times.

> And much they griev'd to see so nigh their Hall,
> The Bird that warn'd St. *Peter* of his Fall;

That he should raise his miter'd Crest on high,
And clap his Wings, and call his Family
To Sacred Rites; and vex th' Etherial Pow'rs
With midnight Mattins, at uncivil Hours:
Nay more, his quiet Neighbours should molest,
Just in the sweetness of their Morning rest.

(ll. 1005–12)

Turning to the Protestant, and specifically Anglican, approach to worship, Dryden leaves little doubt that he has in mind Latitudinarian "contamination" of Christian doctrine, disguised as progress over a "dull" past. The sexual imagery daringly but effectively argues a particular "interest" present in Anglicanism from its inception.

The World was fall'n into an easier way,
This Age knew better, than to Fast and Pray.
Good Sense in Sacred Worship would appear
So to begin, as they might end the year.
Such feats in former times had wrought the falls
Of crowing *Chanticleers* in Cloyster'd Walls.
Expell'd for this, and for their Lands they fled,
And Sister *Partlet* with her hooded head
Was hooted hence, because she would not pray a-bed.
The way to win the restiff World to God,
Was to lay by the Disciplining Rod,
Unnatural Fasts, and Foreign Forms of Pray'r;
Religion frights us with a meen severe.
'Tis Prudence to reform her into Ease,
And put Her in undress to make Her pleas:
A lively Faith will bear aloft the Mind,
And leave the Luggage of Good Works behind.

Such Doctrines in the *Pigeon*-house were taught,
You need not ask how wondrously they wrought;
But sure the common cry was all for these
Whose Life, and Precept both encourag'd Ease.

(ll. 1017–37)

That the Latitudinarians are a primary object of Dryden's attack in the Third Part of *The Hind and the Panther* is obvious. The Fable of the Doves and Pigeons draws to a fitting conclusion with the arrival of the Buzzard, a composite of Gilbert Burnet and William III, to handle the "race of *Chanticleer*" (l. 1113). "Or forc'd by Fear, or by his Profit led, / Or both conjoyn'd" (ll. 1151–52), the Buzzard epitomizes Anglicanism and particularly Latitudinarianism, which has so infected Anglican doctrine that the two fairly are equivalent terms: "Int'rest in all his Actions was discern'd" (l. 1149). Dryden, in fact, devotes many lines in the final part to the Latitudinarians, his charges echoing those he made both at this time[10] and for the rest of his life and recalling as well oppositions felt around the time of his layman's faith. For example, after the Hind informs the spotted Panther "how many sons have you / Who call you mother, whom you never knew!" (ll. 144–45), sons who "gape at rich revenues which you hold, / And fain would nible at your grandame gold" (ll. 148–49) and who, "once possess'd of what with care you save, / . . . wou'd piss upon your grave" (ll. 158–59), she proceeds to a direct assault on the Latitudinarians, establishing at the outset the virtual identity of the part with the whole:

> Your sons of Latitude that court your grace,
> Though most resembling you in form and face,
> Are far the worst of your pretended race.
> . . . .
> Their malice too a sore suspicion brings;
> For though they dare not bark, they snarl at kings:
> Nor blame 'em for intruding in your line,
> Fat Bishopricks are still of right divine.
>
> (ll. 160–62, 169–72)

Following lines on "your new *French* Proselytes" (l. 173), drawn to England by the prospect of just these prosperous benefices, the Hind taxes the Latitudinarians with the inconstancy, malleability, and materialistic self-interest exposed elsewhere in the poem:

Your sons of breadth at home, are much like these,
Their soft and yielding metals run with ease,
They melt, and take the figure of the mould:
But harden, and preserve it best in gold.

(ll. 187–90)

As Dryden presents them, the Latitudinarians embody the
faults and vices that he had been attacking for at least twenty
years and that evidently helped convince him to move from the
Church of England to the Church of Rome. They are also the
most extreme instance of the interest, impurity, and changeable-
ness that Dryden located in the Church of England from the
opening line of *The Hind and the Panther:*

Tax those of int'rest who conform for gain,
Or stay the market of another reign.
Your broad-way sons wou'd never be too nice
To close with *Calvin*, if he paid their price;
But rais'd three steeples high'r, wou'd change their note,
And quit the Cassock for the Canting-coat.

(ll. 227–32)

The lines are prophetic. When such churchmen swore allegiance
to William and Mary, that prophecy seemed confirmed. The
confirmation in turn augmented Dryden's opposition to these
priests.

To Dryden the Renaissance revival of learning and overthrow of ignorance and superstition was an undisputed good.
The plaguing question, as he implied in *Religio Laici*, a powerful
testament to Renaissance and Reformation achievements, was
exactly what to do with the opportunities available for intellectual growth. By 1687, in *The Hind and the Panther*, Dryden's answer is writ large. In that poem appears a corrected humanism,
a humanism subordinate to a deepening Catholic faith.

The mind displayed in *The Hind and the Panther* is generally
content and at peace with itself and God. Gone now are the as-

sertiveness and tension felt in the layman's faith and due in large measure to the "pride" he had not yet subdued. Acceptance, submissiveness, and faith permeate the later poem, affecting even the movement of the verse, itself assured and expressive of contentment. The simplicity of such lines as the following suggests the serenity they fully express, as well as the difference from the earlier Anglican restlessness and striving:

> Rest then, my soul, from endless anguish freed;
> Nor sciences thy guide, nor sense thy creed.
> Faith is the best ensurer of thy bliss;
> The Bank above must fail before the venture miss.
>
> (1:146–49)

With obvious finality, having reached the goal described and sought in *Religio Laici*, Dryden declares, "Good life be now my task: my doubts are done" (1:78).

Secure in his own faith and committed to the Christian promise as traditionally understood, Dryden continues during his Catholic years to lash out at moral turpitude and ungodliness. Certainly he seems more and more distanced from what he calls "This lubrique and adult'rate age" (*To the Pious Memory Of . . . Mrs Anne Killigrew* [1686], l. 63), in which "In Lusts we wallow, and with Pride we swell" (*Britannia Rediviva* [1688], l. 281). Dryden's denunciations of vice and perversion are perhaps more biting than earlier, at least with regard to the clergy's involvement in, and indeed (partial) responsibility for, such corruption.

Though Dryden remained alert to priestly corruption generally, including in the proud and reckless Father Edward Petre of his own church (Martyn in the fable of the swallows' fate), he yet maintains, along with the Hind, that

> Such *Martyns* build in yours, and more than mine:
> Or else an old fanatick Authour lyes
> Who summ'd their Scandals up by Centuries.[11]
>
> (3:654–56)

Indeed, the only significant target of his anticlericalism now is the *de jure* Anglican clergy, whom Dryden views as extending the principles and practices of Latitudinarianism, the growth of which was evidently a major factor in his decision to convert. For encouraging the deposition of James II and the accession of the "usurpers" William and Mary, for making the "Glorious Revolution" secure, and for fostering a climate in which pluralism, schism, and unbelief could thrive,[12] Dryden abusively scored these churchmen throughout the 1690s. The charges become a frequent refrain in plays, poems, and prefaces: the "lib'ral *Clergy*" (*The Hind and the Panther*, 3:252) are self-seeking materialists who completely subvert the priestly function; more interested in advancement and, in many instances, in secular and political offices than in the care of souls, they are all too willing to sacrifice their spiritual vocation for the possibility of lucrative benefices that might come as payment for political services rendered. In them appears all that Dryden had so long opposed in churchmen. So convinced was he of the heinousness of their actions that in the Preface to the *Fables* (1700) he concluded that such Anglican churchmen "have given the last blow to Christianity in this age, by a practice so contrary to their doctrine."[13] The important continuity in Dryden's perception of these churchmen and their principles, from the early 1680s to 1700, bridging his conversion to the Church of Rome, supports the suggestions I offered earlier regarding his change of faith.

Of the plays Dryden wrote in the last ten years of his life only *Don Sebastian* (1690) contains a serious and extended treatment of churchmen; in the other plays, *Amphitryon* (1690), *King Arthur* (1691), *Cleomenes* (1692), and *Love Triumphant* (1694), comments on the clergy appear infrequently and are offhand, rather than dramatically consequential.[14] In *Don Sebastian*, however, through the dramatically significant role given to the Mufti, Dryden devotes considerable attention to the priesthood and the nature of its obligations. The depiction is, first of all, reminiscent of such intriguing priests as those in *The Duke of Guise* several years before. For in the fourth act the Mufti validates Benducar's earlier—and familiar—accusations that he "froths

Treason at his mouth" (I.i.413) and that a Mufti is inevitably "in the way, / When Tumult and Rebellion shou'd be broach'd" (IV.i.67–68). But his particular attempt here to lead the rabble in revolt against the emperor proves unsuccessful, for the mob appears reluctant to follow a mufti: "when his turn is serv'd, he may preach up Loyalty again, and Restitution, that he might have another Snack among us" (IV.iii.154–56).

This only slightly veiled attack on the Anglican clergy is fully exploited elsewhere in the play. Though Scott, following Jeremy Collier, believed that through the Mufti "Dryden has seized an opportunity to deride and calumniate the priesthood of every religion; an opportunity which, I am sorry to say, he seldom fails to use with unjustifiable inveteracy,"[15] the attack is aimed directly at the Anglican clergy. Particularly important, for our purposes, is the lengthy passage in II.i. in which Dryden again treats the responsibilities of the priesthood, recalling similar lines in *The Hind and the Panther* and anticipating the fuller discussion in the "Good Parson" and, by implication, blasting the Latitudinarian churchmen for their materialism, hypocrisy, and willful slighting of their spiritual obligations. The hero Dorax is berating the Mufti:

> Your Heav'n you promise, but our Earth you covet;
> The *Phaethons* of mankind, who fire that World,
> Which you were sent by Preaching but to warm.
> . . . .
>   Now his Zeal yearns,
> To see me burnt; he damns me from his Church,
> Because I wou'd restrain him to his Duty;
> Is not the care of Souls a load sufficient?
> Are not your holy stipends pay'd for this?
> Were you not bred apart from worldly noise,
> To study Souls, their Cures and their Diseases?
> If this be so, we ask you but our own:
> Give us your whole Employment, all your care:
> The Province of the Soul is large enough

To fill up every Cranny of your time,
And leave you much to answer, if one Wretch
Be damn'd by your neglect.

(165–67, 171–82)

Continuing, Dorax centers on the political involvement that results from clerical greed, echoing the position Dryden expressed in *The Indian Emperour* a quarter of a century earlier. The analysis is rather subtle:

Why then these forein thoughts of State-Employments,
Abhorrent to your Function and your Breeding?
Poor droaning Truants of unpractis'd Cells,
Bred in the Fellowship of bearded Boys,
What wonder is it if you know not Men?
Yet there, you live demure, with down-cast Eyes,
And humble as your Discipline requires:
But, when let loose from thence to live at large,
Your little tincture of Devotion dies:
Then Luxury succeeds, and set agog
With a new Scene of yet untasted Joys,
You fall with greedy hunger to the Feast.
Of all your College Vertues, nothing now
But your Original Ignorance remains;
Bloated with Pride, Ambition, Avarice,
You swell, to counsel Kings and govern Kingdoms.

(184–98)

The Mufti feebly interjects, "He prates as if Kings had not Consciences, / And none requir'd Directors but the Crowd" (199–200), to which Dorax replies:

As private men they want you, not as Kings;
Nor wou'd you care t' inspect their publick Conscience,
But that it draws dependencies of Pow'r,
And Earthly Interest which you long to sway.

(201–4)

In having Dorax revile the clergy's role as advisers to the monarchy, Dryden evidently has in mind activities of certain Anglican churchmen during the last years of the Stuart reign. Whatever the exact nature of the activity which prompted this attack, Dorax resumes his anticlerical harangue in the third act, addressing the emperor Muley-Moloch:

> Sir, let me bluntly say, you went too far,
> To trust the Preaching pow'r on State Affairs,
> To him or any Heavenly Demagogue.
> 'Tis a limb lopt from your Prerogative,
> And so much of Heav'ns Image blotted from you.
> (384–88)

Following the Mufti's reply that such churchmen as Wolsey made notable contributions as statesmen, Dorax resumes, clearly distinguishing between the priestly function and the all-too-human men who undertake it, repeating the call Dryden consistently made for the separation of religious interests from state affairs, and warning the emperor of the political dangers in "interested" clerical involvement in civil matters:

> How you triumph in one or two of these,
> Born to be Statesmen, hap'ning to be Church-men:
> Thou call'st 'em holy; so their function was,
> But tell me, *Mufti,* which of 'em were Saints?
> Next, Sir, to you; the summ of all is this;
> Since he claims pow'r from Heav'n, and not from Kings,
> When 'tis his int'rest, he can int'rest Heav'n
> To preach you down. . . .
> (393–400)

His conclusion is direct and blunt:

> Thus Vice and Godliness, prepost'rous pair,
> Ride cheek by joul; but Churchmen hold the Reins.

And, when ere Kings wou'd lower Clergy greatness,
They learn too late what pow'r the Preachers have,
And whose the Subjects are; the *Mufti* knows it. . . .

(413–17)

In addition, of course, to scoring Anglican allegiance to Mammon and calumniating the *de jure* clergy, *Don Sebastian* makes clear through its insistence on the strict separation of church and state that Dryden, like his fellow Catholic Alexander Pope some time later, rejected the idea of papal supremacy in temporal affairs.

In the *Fables,* published in 1700, the year he died, Dryden again turned to the priesthood, its responsibilities, and recent Anglican perversion of those responsibilities. Though these are the overriding concern of "The Character of a Good Parson," and certainly important in "The Cock and the Fox: or, The Tale of the Nun's Priest, from Chaucer," we will do well to begin with the famous Preface, where, in a long and closely reasoned digression, Dryden moves from a discussion of Chaucer's handling of priests to a general defense of the satirical poet as check on clerical corruption. Throughout Dryden implies his similarity to the earlier poet as he attempts for the first time, after some forty years of priest-baiting, a theoretical justification of his own attacks on churchmen. As the reference later on to James Drake suggests, this defense was occasioned, in part at least, by Collier's *Short View of the Immorality and Profaneness of the English Stage,* which singled out Dryden's frequent attacks on the clergy; clearly Dryden was stung by Collier's criticism. After acknowledging with regret Chaucer's "bias towards the opinions of Wickliff," Dryden focuses on his anticlericalism, being careful to distinguish particular churchmen from the priestly function itself. Though he admits that clerical corruption was abundant in Chaucer's time, he implies that the present Anglican clergy is at least equally corrupt and deserving of the satirist's lashes; the faults found in the earlier clergy are precisely those that the "Good Parson" locates in present-day Anglican priests. Yet, he writes, the scandal which is given by particular priests reflects not on the sacred function. Chaucer's Monk, his Canon, and his Friar, took not from the character of his Good Parson. A satirical poet is the check of the laymen on bad priests. We are only to take care that we involve not the innocent with the guilty in the same condemnation.[16] The good cannot be too much honoured, nor the bad too coarsely used; for the corruption of the best becomes the worst. When a clergyman is whipped, his gown is first taken off, by which the dignity of his order is secured. If he be wrongfully accused, he has his action of slander; and 'tis at the poet's peril if he transgress the law. But they will tell us that all kind of satire, though never so well deserved by particular priests, yet brings the whole order into contempt. Is then the peerage of England anything dishonoured when a peer suffers for his treason? If he be libelled, or any way defamed, he has his *scandalum magnatum* to punish the offender. They who use this kind of argument seem to be conscious to themselves of somewhat which has deserved the poet's lash, and are less concerned for their public capacity than for their private; at least there is pride at the bottom of their reasoning. If the faults of men in orders are only to be judged among themselves, they are all in some sort parties; for, since they say the honour of their order is concerned in every member of it, how can we be sure that they will be impartial judges? How far I may be allowed to speak my opinion in this case, I know not. . . . The learned and ingenious Dr Drake has saved me the labour of inquiring into the esteem and reverence which the priests have had of old; and I would rather extend than diminish any part of it: yet I must needs say that when a priest provokes me without any occasion given him, I have no reason, unless it be the charity of a Christian, to forgive him: *prior laesit* is justification sufficient in the civil law. If I answer him in his own language, self-defence, I am sure, must be allowed me; and if I carry it farther, even to a sharp recrimination, somewhat may be indulged to human frailty. Yet my resentment has not wrought so far, but that I have followed Chaucer in his character of a holy man, and have enlarged on that subject with some pleasure, reserving to myself the right, if I shall think fit hereafter, to describe another sort of priests, such as are more easily to be found than the Good Parson; such as have given the last blow to Christianity in this age, by a practice so contrary to their doctrine.[17]

Given the nature of his treatment of priests in the fables themselves, I see no reason to question Dryden's description of at least his present position.

That position is given fullest expression in two of the Chaucerian imitations in the *Fables*. Though Earl Miner has suggested that "The Cock and the Fox" is "an intermittent allegory of the follies of a priest,"[18] the details of that allegory have not, to my knowledge, been worked out, and thus the exact nature of Dryden's treatment of the clergy in this little-known poem has gone undetermined. I can treat the poem here in only the most general way. To begin with, the poem Dryden is "imitating," *The Nun's Priest's Tale*, is itself an allegory with the cock Chanticleer representing the clergy and the widow the church.[19] Of ancient vintage, entering Christian thought by way of the "mystical" glosses on Matthew 26, the typology of the cock as priest was not unknown to Dryden, for in lines 1006 ff. of the Third Part of *The Hind and the Panther* he refers to "The Bird that warn'd St. Peter of his Fall" and proceeds to note, evidently aware of the typological association of the cock with licentiousness, "the falls / Of crowing *Chanticleers* in Cloyster'd Walls." With the help of Dryden's "Moral," which points out that "The Cock and Fox, the Fool and Knave imply" (K, l. 814),[20] the allegory becomes transparent. Specifically, as Miner notes, "Partlet is given to what is apparently private reason; in any event, like the Socinian Fox of *The Hind and the Panther*, she denies the supernatural."[21] Much like the Anglican clergy, irresistibly drawn to the rationalistic positions of the Cambridge Platonists, the Latitudinarians, and men such as Martin Clifford, the proud and lustful Chanticleer is attracted to the disbelieving Partlet. It is precisely this influence, alongside his own vanity and foolishness, that makes Chanticleer-priest an easy prey for the cunning Fox, here representative of Puritanism.[22] "The Cock and the Fox" thus seems to dramatize the grave and somewhat complementary dangers (from Puritanism and excessive reliance on the private reason) to which the Anglican priesthood was exposed, as well as its own cunning, partly inspired by the Fox, which ultimately saves it from being swallowed up. That Chanticleer is able to outwit the Fox and save himself, though not without being further tainted by his enemy's principles, not only reflects Anglican resiliency, adaptability, and impurity but also supports Dryden's claim made twenty years earlier in *The Spanish Fryar* that the clergy are always "wise enough to slip their own necks out of the collar."

The fullest direct treatment Dryden ever gave the priesthood, "The Character of a Good Parson; Imitated from Chaucer, And Inlarg'd," is one of his very rare positive statements on churchmen, as well as one of the last pieces he wrote. At least some of the facts of composition of this "imitation," if not the depth of personal involvement it reveals, are well known. In 1699 Dryden wrote to Samuel Pepys that he had accepted his friend's suggestion of the previous year and had completed this poem based on Chaucer's portrait in the General Prologue of *The Canterbury Tales*.[23] Apparently, however, as early as 1691 Dryden was considering a work dealing in an important way with the clergy, for in August of that year William Walsh inquired of him whether he had "begun ye other design you told mee of ab^t ye priesthood."[24] No such work from this date is extant, or at least known, and it may be that the "Good Parson" is a fulfillment of those earlier plans, perhaps interrupted by more pressing demands, notably the large body of translations then under way, and at the same time the result of Pepys's recent recommendation. In view of the imitation Dryden made, this seems likely.

Whatever the facts of composition, the occasion of the poem seems clear.[25] As has frequently been noted, Dryden describes the political situation confronting the Good Parson in such a way as to leave little doubt that he has in mind the recent revolution. Like so much of Dryden's work after 1688, this poem was occasioned by the actions of the main body of the Anglican clergy during the past several years. In such a passage as the following, where the allegory is obvious, the Good Parson, who is appropriately anonymous, becomes the standard by which the *de jure* clergy's worldliness and ambition are judged and condemned:

> God, saw his Image lively was express'd;
> And his own Work, as in Creation bless'd.
>   The Tempter saw him too, with envious Eye;
> And, as on *Job*, demanded leave to try.
> He took the time when *Richard* was depos'd:
> And High and Low, with happy *Harry* clos'd.
> This Prince, tho' great in Arms, the Priest withstood:
> Near tho' he was, yet not the next of Blood.
> Had *Richard* unconstrain'd, resign'd the Throne: ⎫
> A King can give no more than is his own: ⎬
> The Title stood entail'd, had *Richard* had a Son. ⎭
>   Conquest, an odious Name, was laid aside,
> Where all submitted; none the Battle try'd.
> The senseless Plea of Right by Providence,
> Was, by a flatt'ring Priest, invented since:
> And lasts no longer than the present sway;
> But justifies the next who comes in play.
>   The People's Right remains; let those who dare
> Dispute their Pow'r, when they the Judges are.
>   He join'd not in their Choice; because he knew
> Worse might, and often did from Change ensue.
> Much to himself he thought; but little spoke:
> And, Undepriv'd, his Benefice forsook.[26]
>
> (K, ll. 104–26)

Throughout the poem the Parson's selflessness and fidelity to the Christian and, especially, priestly ideal evoke by contrast the implied picture of the self-seeking Anglican clergy we encountered in *The Hind and the Panther* and *Don Sebastian*. But the Good Parson stands in striking contrast not only with the *de jure* clergy but also with the countless other churchmen Dryden had been criticizing for at least forty years. He reminds one somewhat of Dryden's brief description of "*Zadock* the Priest" in *Absalom and Achitophel,* praiseworthy for "shunning Power and Place" (l. 864). Thus while Dryden's immediate, satirical interest is in those priests of the Church of England who, by their recent actions, seemed to men of his persuasion to demonstrate abandonment of the traditional principles of their calling, the Good Parson emerges in his own right as Dryden's ideal churchman.[27] Dryden's interests in the "Good Parson" are so broad and multifarious that only a few of the numerous issues taken up in the poem have specific reference to the situation involving the *de jure* churchmen.

The various qualities both Dryden and Chaucer ascribe to the Good Parson are those lacking in the countless examples of bad priests the later poet lambastes, including, of course, the recently blameworthy priests of the Established Church. Considerably enlarging and developing Chaucer's portrait (the later version almost triples the length of the original), Dryden presents an extended account of the Parson, which depicts him as poor but learned, unambitious, charitable, indeed self-sacrificing, careful to present a good example to his parishioners, and far and happily removed from the worlds and interests of clerical and political intrigue. Dryden's Parson rejects possibilities for advancement, preferment, and tempting benefices, believing that his primary obligation is to his flock and their spiritual well-being.

> True Priests, he said, and Preachers of the Word,
> Were only Stewards of their Soveraign Lord;
> Nothing was theirs; but all the publick Store:
> Intrusted Riches, to relieve the Poor.

Who, shou'd they steal, for want of his Relief,
He judg'd himself Accomplice with the Thief.

(K, ll. 54–59)

Like the above, the following passage vividly realizes the Parson's distance from such corrupt churchmen as those lashed in *The Hind and the Panther* and earlier in *Absalom and Achitophel*, where, already, Anglican priests are said to be primarily interested in "the Fleece [which] accompanies the Flock" (l. 129):

His Preaching much, but more his Practice wrought;
(A living Sermon of the Truths he taught;)
For this by Rules severe his Life he squar'd:
That all might see the Doctrin which they heard.
For Priests, he said, are Patterns for the rest:
(The Gold of Heav'n, who bear the God Impress'd:)
But when the precious Coin is kept unclean,
The Soveraign's Image is no longer seen.
If they be foul, on whom the People trust,
Well may the baser Brass, contract a Rust.

(K, ll. 77–86)

Expanding details and adding nuances from the beginning, Dryden ranges widely in the poem, expatiating on various matters pertaining to the priesthood that interest him. Whereas, for example, Chaucer simply notes that his parson

. . . Cristes gospel trewely wolde preche;
His parisshens devoutly wolde he teche.
Benygne he was, and wonder diligent,
And in adversitee ful pacient,[28]

Dryden devotes some thirty lines to a description of the Parson's homiletics (ll. 11–41). In this passage the Parson is likened to a singer and musician using his art to capture his audience's attention and thence to move them in the desired way. In his sermon the Parson both preaches and exemplifies love. Kindly and merciful himself, he teaches "the Gospel rather than the Law" (K, l. 30) and dwells on "the Joys of Heav'n" (K, l. 27). Differing, however, from Tillotson and other "Latitude-men," the Parson does not "dulcify" Christian doctrine; his is not an *"easie* God" who can be satisfied simply by "Good Sense in Sacred Worship." Rather, both the Parson and the God whose Will he implements are like the mirror-image represented in David in *Absalom and Achitophel:* they are figures of strength, authority, and justice who govern by "native mercy" as they prefer but who will, when necessary, draw "the Sword of Justice." Unlike, therefore, the "easie" benevolists who brought heaven closer to home while keeping hell at a safe distance, including those satirized in the Fable of the Doves and Pigeons in *The Hind and the Panther* (esp. ll. 1005–37), the Parson preaches not only "the Joys of Heav'n" but also the "Pains of Hell" (K, l. 27). He thus achieves an ideal, for while preaching and representing a God of both mercy and justice, he avoids not only the easiness Dryden consistently associated with Latitudinarianism but also the opposite "extreme," such superstition, fear, and tyranny as Pope later repudiated in the third epistle of *An Essay on Man* (ll. 241 ff.). Dryden writes, "He taught the Gospel rather than the Law: / And forc'd himself to drive; but lov'd to draw" (K, ll. 30–31). Accordingly, Dryden distinguishes the Parson's particular zeal from the methods of those who—in Samuel Butler's terms—make the pulpit a "drum ecclesiastick," for the Parson believes that

> Lightnings and Thunder (Heav'ns Artillery)
> As Harbingers before th' Almighty fly:
> Those, but proclaim his Stile, and disappear;
> The stiller Sound succeeds; and God is there.
> (K, ll. 38–41)

One of Dryden's major points in "The Character of a Good Parson" is that implied throughout his writings: religion thrives or languishes according to the example set by its adherents, perhaps the most important of whom in this regard are priests. Unlike many Anglican churchmen of the late seventeenth century (at least as Dryden viewed them), the Good Parson perfectly mirrors the doctrine he represents, and in the poem Dryden stresses practice and example: "His Preaching much, but more his Practice wrought; / (A living Sermon of the Truths he taught)." Dryden distinguishes his ideal Parson, then, not only from the Latitudinarians, whose practice, he thought, belied their teaching as Christian clergy, and zealous Calvinists, but also those from whom the latter perhaps took their cue, the disputatious Scholastic theologians, who tended to make religion a matter of dogmas and syllogisms. With his stress on practice and brilliantly effective rhetoric the Parson exhibits the humanistic virtues missing in both medieval and latter-day dialecticians; this depiction probably reflects in part the earlier influence on Dryden of the layman's faiths.

As these themes are being developed in the poem, a significant change occurs in Dryden's narrative method, for at lines 32 ff. he rather unobtrusively steps out from behind the Parson and, ceasing to make his own points through his character, begins to speak directly:

> For Fear but freezes Minds; but Love, like Heat,
> Exhales the Soul sublime, to seek her Native Seat.
>   To Threats, the stubborn Sinner oft is hard:
> Wrap'd in his Crimes, against the Storm prepar'd;
> But, when the milder Beams of Mercy play,
> He melts, and throws his cumb'rous Cloak away.

In later passages Dryden also speaks directly for himself. It is, for example, the poet who interprets the life and teachings of Christ in lines 88–97, proposing them as the pattern for all churchmen to follow and implicitly pointing up the striking contrast between his poverty and the shameful worldliness of so many, if not all, churchmen, which is thereby powerfully censured:

His Saviour came not with a gawdy Show;
Nor was his Kingdom of the World below.
Patience in Want, and Poverty of Mind,
These Marks of Church and Churchmen he design'd, }
And living taught; and dying left behind.
The Crown he wore was of the pointed Thorn:
In Purple he was Crucify'd, not born.
They who contend for Place and high Degree,
Are not his Sons, but those of *Zebadee.*

In the overtly political section of the poem (ll. 105 ff.), for which there is no precedent in the original, Dryden editorializes once more, urging the right of the next of kin to the throne and blaming the clergy for undermining allegiance to the idea of the Succession (see esp. ll. 115–19). What Dryden's editorializing reveals is that the Chaucerian "imitation" has provided the opportunity to express his personal opinions on a number of points of lasting importance to him. The resulting discursiveness may detract from the value of the poem as poem, but it provides welcome insight into Dryden's religious thought at the end of his life.

The strength of Dryden's continuing interest in the priesthood is nowhere better illustrated than in the final four lines of the poem, where he uses the first-person singular for the first time. In a deceptively quiet tone he brings the poem and its discussion of the priesthood to a decisive close, one that is different from Chaucer's. Whereas the earlier poet merely claims that there exists no better priest than his parson ("A bettre preest I trowe that nowher noon ys"), Dryden asserts that all others were far from even approaching the Parson's Christlike standards:

In deference to his Virtues, I forbear
To shew you, what the rest in Orders were:
This Brillant, is so Spotless, and so Bright,
He needs no Foyl: But shines by his own proper Light.

Patterned on no one in particular,[29] the Good Parson is a composite of the various priestly qualities that had so long stood behind Dryden's vehement denunciations of clerical failure but that had never been fully and directly articulated. In thus presenting an ideal priest, Dryden has at last brought to the forefront the standards implied in the negative pictures that as a whole constitute his lifelong treatment of priests. The poem is a fitting conclusion to Dryden's focal concern with the priesthood. As Dryden makes clear his Catholic position on the priesthood, he also reveals much about his own later general religious thinking, for what the Good Parson embodies is the Christian religion as Dryden thought it should be interpreted and practiced. The picture of Christianity that emerges from the poem, however, is not discontinuous with Dryden's thinking as far back as *Religio Laici*.

Both continuity and change, in fact, appear in this final treatment of the priesthood. If the standards now stressed are essentially those implied twenty years earlier, it is nevertheless the case that Dryden could not then be positive. Having moved from Protestantism with its fundamental insistence on the priesthood of all believers to a religion that insists on the power, authority, and indeed primacy of the church as organization, Dryden can now accept the sacerdotalism essential to and characteristic of Roman Catholicism. The difference lies finally not in a supposed or real necessity as a Catholic to curb his anticlericalism but rather in the transformation that Dryden had himself undergone, making whatever changes that appear in his treatment of priests completely self-induced. As *The Hind and the Panther* establishes, he had conquered the pride, willfulness, and self-assertiveness that, despite his best efforts, characterizes even *Religio Laici* and as a result can "her alone for my Directour take / Whom thou hast promis'd never to forsake!" Having, in other words, realized the depth of his insufficiency, he can accept the church as the needed director he had vainly tried to be himself. Such acceptance need not mean, as it did not for Erasmus, silence as to undoubted abuse and corruption in the church and her servants, nor repudiation of earlier, less discriminating, and more "interested" attacks on the clergy. Dryden can therefore accept the Roman Catholic Church and continue to lash priests, whether of an opposing faith or his own, when they fail to meet the unblemished standards represented in the Good Parson. That poem, then, should not be viewed as a recantation of earlier, abusive treatments of priests; rather, it is a continuation, with some important modifications, of a deeply felt need to serve as a check on bad priests, perhaps the main difference being that in 1700 Dryden does so in order to elevate the priesthood, not to minimize it. Quite clearly, he does in "The Character of a Good Parson" what he claims in the Preface to the *Fables:* he carefully distinguishes between the priestly order itself and the fallen, fallible human beings who comprise that order;[30] at the same time he testifies, powerfully, to the potential for spiritual and human service that rests with the priesthood. With a noticeable mellowness and depth of understanding not apparent earlier, the "Good Parson" marks the completion of the movement we have traced in Dryden from individualistic advocate of the rights of the laity to a devout adherent to the vast and sustaining organization that claims to be the catholic church.

Notes

Chapter 1

1. Bredvold, *The Intellectual Milieu of John Dryden: Studies in Some Aspects of Seventeenth-Century Thought* (1934; rpt. Ann Arbor: University of Michigan Press, 1956).

2. The list is impressive; it includes James M. Osborn, *John Dryden: Some Biographical Facts and Problems* (1940; rpt. Gainesville: University of Florida Press, 1965); George R. Noyes, ed., *The Poetical Works of John Dryden*, 2d ed. (Boston: Houghton Mifflin, 1950); Bonamy Dobrée, *John Dryden* (London: Longmans, 1956); and Charles E. Ward, *The Life of John Dryden* (Chapel Hill: University of North Carolina Press, 1961).

3. Fujimura, "Dryden's *Religio Laici*: An Anglican Poem," *PMLA* 76 (1961): 205–17, and Chiasson, "Dryden's Apparent Scepticism in *Religio Laici*," *Harvard Theological Review* 54 (1961): 207–21.

4. Harth, *Contexts of Dryden's Thought* (Chicago: University of Chicago Press, 1968).

5. Budick, *Dryden and the Abyss of Light: A Study of "Religio Laici" and "The Hind and the Panther,"* Yale Studies in English, vol. 174 (New Haven, Conn.: Yale University Press, 1970), p. 47.

6. McHenry, "Dryden's *Religio Laici*: An Augustan Drama of Ideas," *Enlightenment Essays* 4 (1973): 60–64, and "The Importance of Right Reason in Dryden's Conversion," *Mosaic* 7 (1974): 69–86; Empson, "Dryden's Apparent Scepticism," *Essays in Criticism* 20 (1970): 172–81, and "A Deist Tract by Dryden," *Essays in Criticism* 25 (1975): 74–100.

7. Harth, *Contexts of Dryden's Thought*, p. 96. In pp. 42–47, Harth presents the argument I have sketched. Despite Dryden's own claim to the contrary (e.g., "Thus have I made my own Opinions clear," 1. 451), Harth contends that the voice we hear in the poem is not Dryden's but that of "a rhetorical posture assumed for the occasion"; as an apologist, he continues, Dryden's task was merely "to borrow his arguments from

elsewhere, to enhance them with the power of poetic expression, and to fashion them into a poetic discourse whereby men may be 'reason'd into Truth'" (pp. 46, 42). The effect of approaching Dryden as rhetorical strategist in this way is to separate *Religio Laici*, as well as *The Hind and the Panther*, from the author and his other work and so to restrict excessively and unnecessarily the conclusions we can legitimately draw about his personal opinions. Indeed, the argument is that these two poems alone constitute "the primary contexts in which [Dryden's] religious thought is to be understood" (p. viii). The relevance of the poet's other works to an understanding of his religious positions is thus denied or at best minimized. If the points expressed in lives and prefaces may be of some help, even though "neither systematic nor inherently important," the ideas appearing in the plays are said to be "irrelevant to a study of Dryden's thought" because "ideas of this kind are to be explained, not by reference to Dryden's own beliefs, but by an understanding of the part they play in revealing character or in supplying the motivation for dramatic action" (p. vii). Despite Harth, as Budick and others acknowledge, we can, of course, determine a playwright's stand on the ideas he presents. Moreover, Dryden's religious thought entails a variety of issues, not all of them overtly religious. Despite the claim to the contrary, in Dryden religion is not an isolated matter with easily defined limits but rather is bound up with and inseparable from everything else in life. Study of Dryden's religious thought must, therefore, involve not only *Religio Laici* and *The Hind and the Panther* but also the well-known satires and political poems, the plays, the various prose works, and such imitations as "The Character of a Good Parson." I have discussed objections to Harth and others and proposed an alternative in "Dryden's *Religio Laici*: A Reappraisal," *Studies in Philology* 75 (1978): 347–70.

8. Samuel Johnson, *Lives of the English Poets*, ed. G. B. Hill (Oxford, 1905), 1:442; Smith, *John Dryden* (Cambridge: Cambridge University Press, 1950), pp. 60–61. The view that in *Religio Laici* Dryden is trying to work out his own problems does not preclude the likelihood that he is also trying to affect current conditions.

9. Hoffman, *John Dryden's Imagery* (Gainesville: University of Florida Press, 1962), pp. 55–71.

10. P. 7. Noting Dryden's treatment of priests in *Absalom and Achitophel*, J. R. concludes that the poet "made them to be all alike Cheats and Impostors . . . by Priest-Craft he makes no distinction, but takes them all in from *Dan* to *Bersheba*, as if no Religion could be good where a Priest was concern'd" (p. 6).

11. Two of these, those by (apparently) Lord Vaughan and Thomas

Creech, introduced *Religio Laici* in the first edition as well as in the second issue, also 1682, and the 1683 edition, to the latter of which was added another poem (by Roscommon); a fourth—anonymous—poem appeared in Tonson's *Miscellany Poems* in 1684. From the Scott-Saintsbury edition at the end of the nineteenth century until 1971 the introductory poems were not reprinted with *Religio Laici*. James and Helen Kinsley then printed three of the poems complete, as well as part of Roscommon's, in *Dryden: The Critical Heritage* (London: Routledge and Kegan Paul), and in 1972 the introductory poems were included in an appendix to the second volume of the California Edition of the *Works* (to which my citations refer). Unlike Harth, Budick glances at the introductory poems. On the authorship of the first introductory poem see Richard H. Perkinson, "A Note on Dryden's *Religio Laici*," *Philological Quarterly* 28 (1949):517–18.

12. Though all sixteen works testify in varying degrees to the growth of laicism, I omit from those among them which oppose the layman's to the clergy's faith the 1688 *Religio Laici* by J. R. and *Religio Militis*, both of which derive from the current political situation and are specifically and principally addressed to it. Moreover, whereas the works by Browne and Hildesley, for example, express the faith of a layman who happens to be a medical man or lawyer, *Religio Militis* is exclusively "the religion of a soldeir [*sic*]." I have likewise omitted from the layman's faith classification *The Lay-Christians Obligation*, *The Lay-mans Opinion*, and *The Lay-Mans Answer to the Lay-Mans Opinion*, all published in 1687 and all aimed as direct replies to polemics written by opponents in the current controversies. For reasons made clear by their titles I have also omitted *The Lay-Divine: or, The simple House-preaching Taylor; Who Whilest by his pretended Enthusiasms he would seem to divert his Brethren from the way to Hell, spreads his Banner of party-coloured Heresies to lead them thither* (London, 1647), and Edmund Hickeringill's *The Lay-Clergy: or, The Lay-Elder. In a Short Essay in Answer To this Query; Whether it be Lawful for Persons in Holy Orders to Exercise Temporal Offices, Honours, Jurisdictions and Authorities* (London, 1695). Works with similar titles appeared in the early eighteenth century (e.g., *Concio Laici*), but I have found none with the characteristics of the layman's faith as I have defined it.

Herbert's *Religio Laici*, Browne's *Religio Medici*, and Mackenzie's *Religio Stoici* have all been mentioned as either sources or models for Dryden's poem; see Smith, *John Dryden*, p. 62; *The Poems of John Dryden*, ed. James Kinsley, 4 vols. (Oxford: Clarendon Press, 1958), 4:1933; Budick, *Dryden and the Abyss of Light*, p. 14. Harth refers in passing to a "tradition" of such works but is apparently unfamiliar with the works comprising it. Though he mentions only Lord Herbert's tract, Franklin L.

Baumer has helpfully discussed the seventeenth century's search for a layman's faith; see *Religion and the Rise of Scepticism* (New York: Harcourt, Brace, 1960), pp. 230–92.

13. Blount, *Religio Laici* (London, 1683), pp. 25–26; cf. pp. 2–3, 19, 22–23. His remark that his own work is "a Continuance" of Dryden's poem appears at sigs. Allr-Allv.

14. Sir George Mackenzie, *Religio Stoici* (Edinburgh, 1665), p. 54. See also p. 39.

15. *Lord Herbert of Cherbury's "De Religione Laici,"* ed. and trans. Harold R. Hutcheson, Yale Studies in English, vol. 98 (New Haven, Conn.: Yale University Press, 1944), p. 123. Apparently *Religio Laici* was the title Lord Herbert intended for this work; see Herbert G. Wright, "An Unpublished Manuscript by Lord Herbert of Cherbury Entitled 'Religio Laici,'" *Modern Language Review* 28 (1933):295–307.

16. *Lord Herbert of Cherbury's "De Religione Laici,"* pp. 127, 121.

17. Blount, *Religio Laici*, p. 87; Mackenzie, *Religio Stoici*, p. 141. Elsewhere Mackenzie writes, "Since discretion opened my eyes, I have alwayes judg'd it necessary for a Christian, to look oftener to his *Practice of Piety*, then to his *Confession of Faith*" (sig. A7^r). See also Mark Hildesley, *Religio Jurisprudentis* (London, 1685), pp. 18–19.

18. *The Lay-Man's Religion* (London, 1690), p. 5; the laicism here, it should be noted, is mild and controlled. Besides those specifically cited above, other works belonging to the layman's faith tradition include J. Botrie's *Religio Jurisconsulti* (1649) and Benjamin Bridgewater's *Religio Bibliopolae* (1691), the latter done "In Imitation of Dr Browns *Religio Medici.*"

19. Harth cites the Preface as support of his claim that Dryden's intended audience is "exclusively" Anglican, but the points he adduces, including that Dryden mentions having borrowed "helps" from Anglican divines and that he notes his precaution in showing the manuscript to a man "indefatigably zealous in the service of the Church and State," prove little. Such stated precaution appears in works specifically addressed to a diversified audience. Mackenzie, for example, subtitled his *Religio Stoici* as follows: *With a Friendly Addresse to the Phanaticks of all Sects and Sorts* and (yet) comments in terms Dryden echoes: "There are some expressions in it, which censure may force to speak otherwayes then they have in commission; yet none of them got room in this Discourse, untill they first gave an account of their design to a most pious and learned Divine. . . . As this Discourse intends, for the Divines of our Church, all respect; so all that is in it, is most freely submitted to their censure" (p. 144). Harth's final point is that Dryden uses the first-person plural in referring to Anglicans. This is sometimes true, for Dry-

den is writing as both layman and Anglican. It is worth noting, however, that the unorthodox frequently used the first-person plural in order to insinuate bonds between themselves and Anglican readers; see, for example, the Deist Anthony Collins's *Priestcraft in Perfection* (1710) and *A Discourse of Free-Thinking* (1713).

20. *"Of Dramatic Poesy" and Other Critical Essays*, ed. George Watson (New York: Dutton, 1962), 1:138; hereafter cited as *Essays*.

21. Cf. Mackenzie, *Religio Stoici*, p. 144.

22. I assume the "Friend" was a churchman, as do other commentators. The name most frequently suggested is John Tillotson; see Smith, *John Dryden*, p. 88; *The Poems of John Dryden*, ed. Kinsley, 4:1933; and David R. Brown, "Dryden's 'Religio Laici' and the 'Judicious and Learned Friend,'" *Modern Language Review* 56 (1961):66–69. But since Tillotson was a Latitudinarian and Dryden was by 1682 suspicious of that position, I doubt this.

23. Ferne, *Of the Division between the English and Romish Church upon the Reformation* (London, 1652), pp. 49–50.

24. Cf. Budick, *Dryden and the Abyss of Light*, who describes Dryden's position here as follows: "The Church's view of essentials should neither be accepted privately nor disputed publicly when it seems mistaken to the individual" (p. 157).

25. Harth, *Contexts of Dryden's Thought*, p. 224; Whitby, *An Answer to Sure Footing* (Oxford, 1666), p. 61.

26. *Religio Clerici* (London, 1681), pp. 86, 133–34, sig. A4^r.

27. *Essays*, 2:282.

Chapter 2

1. *The Works of John Dryden*, ed. Sir Walter Scott, rev. and corr. George Saintsbury (Edinburgh, 1883–1892), 1:256; hereafter cited as Scott-Saintsbury. For a different view of the "false lights," see Budick, *Dryden and the Abyss of Light*, pp. 27–28. Though Budick devotes a chapter to the "early theological opinions," he gives only scattered references to a few prose works and a couple of plays.

2. The charge is made by, among others, Robert Gould in *The Laureat* (London, 1687), p. 2. A record of Dryden's baptism on 14 August 1631 has, however, been discovered; see Osborn, *John Dryden*, pp. 285–86.

3. Scott-Saintsbury, 1:32 n.

4. Malone, "An Account of the Life and Writings of the Author," in *The Critical and Miscellaneous Prose Works of John Dryden* (London, 1800), p. 23.

5. Scott-Saintsbury, 1:31–32.

6. Steven N. Zwicker too believes that "the importance of the Puritan background to Dryden's thought should not be underestimated" (*Dryden's Political Poetry: The Typology of King and Nation* [Providence, R.I.: Brown University Press, 1972], p. 130). See also George McFadden, *Dryden the Public Writer: 1660–1685* (Princeton: Princeton University Press, 1978), p. 259; this book appeared after my own study was all but finished.

7. *Calendar of State Papers, Domestic Series, 1603–1610* (London, 1880), p. 200; "John Dod" in *Dictionary of National Biography*. See also Ward, *The Life of John Dryden*, p. 6.

8. Scott-Saintsbury, 1:30 n.; Osborn, *John Dryden*, pp. 139–40.

9. Ward, *The Life of John Dryden*, p. 5.

10. Malone, "An Account," p. 23. Scott cites John Walker's description in his *Sufferings of the Clergy* (Scott-Saintsbury, 1:32 n.).

11. Ward, *The Life of John Dryden*, p. 9.

12. From Walker's *Sufferings of the Clergy*, quoted in Scott-Saintsbury, 1:30 n. On Dryden as a government employee between 1656 and 1658, see Osborn, *John Dryden*, p. 184.

13. See Ward's *Vindiciae Academiarum* (London, 1654), to which John Wilkins contributed a preface.

14. Harth, *Contexts of Dryden's Thought*, p. 17.

15. Ibid., p. 20.

16. Mark H. Curtis, *Oxford and Cambridge in Transition, 1558–1642* (Oxford: Clarendon Press, 1959), p. 258.

17. The "Ode to the Royal Society," ll. 41, 46, published in Sprat's *History of the Royal Society* in 1667. Dryden's own procedure in the poem is inductive, his noting of particular details paralleling the accumulation of evidence done by the scientists.

18. Harth, *Contexts of Dryden's Thought*, p. 24.

19. Edward Pechter, *Dryden's Classical Theory of Literature* (Cambridge: Cambridge University Press, 1975), p.113.

20. *Essays*, 1:26. See Richard Foster Jones, *Ancients and Moderns: A Study of the Rise of the Scientific Movement in Seventeenth-Century England*, 2d ed. (St. Louis: Washington University Press, 1961), esp. p. xii.

21. *Essays*, 1:148.

22. Harth, *Contexts of Dryden's Thought*, pp. 29–30.

23. *Essays*, 1:169.

24. *Annus Mirabilis* was published after Dryden's name was dropped from the rolls of the Royal Society on 29 October 1666 for nonpayment of dues. As Bredvold has shown, this was not the result of any change

in attitude regarding either the Society or the new science; see "Dryden and Waller as Members of the Royal Society," *PMLA* 46 (1931): 954–57, a reply to Claude Lloyd, "John Dryden and the Royal Society," *PMLA* 45 (1930): 967–76.

25. McKeon, *Politics and Poetry in Restoration England: The Case of Dryden's "Annus Mirabilis"* (Cambridge, Mass.: Harvard University Press, 1975), p. 278.

26. Ibid., pp. 152, 247, 280–81.

27. Zwicker shrewdly argues that Dryden's "political typology grows from a distinct literary tradition, finding a base in progressivist historiography and a hermeneutical foundation in Luther's Reformation theology rather than in medieval christocentric theology"; in the 1660s and 1670s, according to this argument, Dryden's "faith in the nation as a covenanted people" reflects his "Protestant reliance on politics as a redemptive instrument" (*Dryden's Political Poetry*, pp. 17, 102–3). Zwicker finds a marked change in Dryden's thought in the 1680s.

28. S. L. Bethell, *The Cultural Revolution of the Seventeenth Century* (London: Dennis Dobson, 1951), p. 65. Saintsbury thought Dryden "had a strong dash of the . . . latitudinarianism of his university" (Scott-Saintsbury, 18:321). See also *A Brief Account of the New Sect of Latitude-Men Together with some Reflections upon the New Philosophy. By S. P. of Cambridge* (London, 1662), sig. A2ʳ, pp. 14 ff.

29. Gerald R. Cragg, *Reason and Authority in the Eighteenth Century* (Cambridge: Cambridge University Press, 1964), p. 28.

30. As indicated above in the Textual Note appended to the Preface, I have cited the California Edition of the *Works* wherever available. Regarding the plays, all citations of *The Wild Gallant, The Indian Emperour,* and *Tyrannick Love* are from this edition, as are those later on to *Don Sebastian,* and will be indicated in the text by act, scene, and line number; references to all other plays are to the Scott-Saintsbury edition and will be cited in the text by act and scene only.

Bruce King has argued that the source of Catherine's argument is John Tillotson; see "Dryden, Tillotson, and *Tyrannic Love,*" *Review of English Studies* 16 (1965): 364–77. Such points as I have quoted were, however, widespread and by no means peculiar to Tillotson.

31. See Pierre Legouis, "La religion dans l'oeuvre de Dryden avant 1682," *Revue Anglo-Américaine* 9 (1932): 529; Bredvold, *The Intellectual Milieu of John Dryden,* p. 112. See also A. W. Verrall, *Lectures on Dryden* (Cambridge: Cambridge University Press, 1914), p. 150.

32. Anne T. Barbeau has similarly noted that in the heroic dramas "Dryden invites his audience to a tolerant appraisal of their fellowman;

he suggests that incorrect thinking, not wicked hearts, brings about re-
bellions or tyrannies" (*The Intellectual Design of John Dryden's Heroic Plays*
[New Haven, Conn.: Yale University Press, 1970], p. 9).

33. Budick, *Dryden and the Abyss of Light*, p. 28.

34. As William P. Holden has remarked, whereas Puritans were vo-
ciferous in denouncing the ignorance, dishonesty, lechery, and greed of
the clergy, "the Roman Catholic or the Anglican [tended to accept] an
amount of corruption as the inevitable characteristic of an institution
which, if of divine inspiration, is of merely human constitution" (*Anti-
Puritan Satire 1572–1642*, Yale Studies in English, vol. 126 [New Haven,
Conn.: Yale University Press, 1954], p. 9). Of course, Dryden's firm and
lasting conviction regarding the supremacy of the crown in state affairs
marks a clear break with Calvinist thought.

35. Earlier in the poem he lamented that the treacherous Bernhard
von Galen, England's only ally in the Second Dutch War, "should teach
the *English* first / That fraud and avarice in the Church could reign!" (ll.
147–48).

36. For reasons too numerous and complex to detail here the seventeenth century was widely anticlerical. Complaints about the low repute
in which the clergy was held appear frequently, perhaps the best-
known example being John Eachard's *Grounds and Occasions of the Contempt of the Clergy* (1670). I have canvassed this problem in "Dryden and
the Clergy" (Ph.D. diss., University of Virginia, 1969).

37. Barbeau, *The Intellectual Design of John Dryden's Heroic Plays*,
pp. 61, 63.

38. Cf. Barbeau's point that in the heroic plays Dryden insists "that
the laws which are imposed by the state should not be rated higher than
conscience, that is, the private moral impulse of each subject" (ibid.,
p. 16). The discussion in *Tyrannick Love* between Maximin and Por-
phyrius on conscience and polity (IV.i.) seems to support the point.

Chapter 3

1. Various changes in Dryden around 1677 have been noted, but no
satisfactory explanation for them has yet been made. Indeed, one can
only speculate, since during these years Dryden wrote little and that
primarily dramatic. My own suggestions regarding these changes will
appear principally in Chapter Five.

2. See, for instance, his claim in "The Grounds of Criticism in Tragedy" (1679) that "'Tis the moral that directs the whole action of the play

to one centre; and that action or fable is the example built upon the moral, which confirms the truth of it to our experience" (*Essays*, 1:248).

3. For helpful discussions of the effects of changing conceptions of man on satirical modes see Ronald Paulson, *The Fictions of Satire* (Baltimore: Johns Hopkins Press, 1967), and P. K. Elkin, *The Augustan Defence of Satire* (Oxford: Clarendon Press, 1973).

4. Pechter, *Dryden's Classical Theory of Literature*, p. 166. I am indebted at several points to Pechter's discussion of *Mac Flecknoe*.

5. Ibid.

6. *Essays*, 1:230, 246. See also 1:260, as well as the Prologue to *Aureng-Zebe*, ll. 13–14, and the Prologue to *Oedipus*, l. 22.

7. *Works*, 17 (*Prose 1668–1691: "An Essay of Dramatic Poesie" and Shorter Works*, ed. Samuel H. Monk and A. E. Wallace Maurer [Berkeley: University of California Press, 1971]):437, 227. The editors recognize that earlier Dryden "had acknowledged progress" (436–37).

8. Compare Dryden's lavish praise of the city's "true Loyalty, invincible Courage and unshaken Constancy" in the dedication to it of *Annus Mirabilis* and the very different picture of it here and in *The Medall*.

9. In "A Parallel Betwixt Painting and Poetry," *Essays*, 2:183. For a concise description of Shadwell's dramatic principles, see *Works*, 2 (*Poems 1681–1684*, ed. H. T. Swedenberg, Jr. [Berkeley: University of California Press, 1972]):306–7.

10. Aubrey Williams, discussing a similar passage in Pope's *Essay on Criticism* in the first volume of the Twickenham Edition of the *Poems*, which volume he and E. Audra edited, *Pastoral Poetry and "An Essay on Criticism"* (New Haven, Conn.: Yale University Press, 1961), p. 220. Cf. the following from "A Parallel Betwixt Painting and Poetry": "the way to please being to imitate nature, both the poets and the painters in ancient times, and in the best ages, have studied her; and from the practice of both these arts, the rules have been drawn by which we are instructed how to please, and to compass that end which they obtained by following their example. For nature is still the same in all ages, and can never be contrary to herself" (*Essays*, 2:191).

11. Werner Jaeger, *Paideia: The Ideals of Greek Culture* (Oxford: Basil Blackwell, 1939), 1:107.

12. Budick, *Poetry of Civilization: Mythopoeic Displacement in the Verse of Milton, Dryden, Pope, and Johnson* (New Haven, Conn.: Yale University Press, 1974).

13. Largely on the basis of comments by Dryden's enemies, E. S. de Beer has claimed that the increase was due to the poet's desire for revenge on the Anglican clergy for having recently denied him either or-

dination or an Oxford post ("Dryden's Anti-Clericalism," *Notes and Queries* 179 [1940]:254–57). Dryden himself explicitly denied ever seeking orders (in the Preface to the *Fables, Essays*, 2:292). For further discussion of the point see my essay "The Function and Significance of the Priest in Dryden's *Troilus and Cressida*," *Texas Studies in Literature and Language* 13 (1971):29–37.

14. Collier, *A Short View of the Immorality and Profaneness of the English Stage* (London, 1698), p. 120.

15. Though *Oedipus* (1679) and *The Kind Keeper* (1680) allude frequently to the familiar clerical sins of self-interest, greed, and hypocrisy, these remarks, like those tossed off in *The Wild Gallant* and *The Assignation*, are extraneous to the main dramatic action.

16. See J. Douglas Canfield, "The Jewel of Great Price: Mutability and Constancy in Dryden's *All for Love*," *ELH* 42 (1975):38–59. See also my essay "Serapion's Function in *All for Love*," *Ball State University Forum* 19 (1978):35–37.

17. Zwicker makes a similar point in *Dryden's Political Poetry*, pp. 102–3.

18. The attitudes and actions of Calchas upon the loss of his tiara, as he himself expresses them, are similar to the motives attributed to Dryden after he was supposedly rebuffed by the Anglican clergy. Might Dryden have created this situation as a reply to the charges brought against him? Certainly *Troilus and Cressida* condemns the priest for having done in effect what Dryden was accused of. I suggest that Calchas's lines provide a valuable insight into Dryden's view of the attitude he has been accused of having and cast further doubt on de Beer's argument. For further discussion, see Atkins, "The Function and Significance of the Priest."

19. By omitting the scene in which Shakespeare showed Calchas beseeching the Greek leaders to arrange an exchange for his daughter (*The Tragedy of Troilus and Cressida*, III.iii.), Dryden strengthens the impression created by the reunion scene he added that the priest cares very little for Cressida.

20. Whether or not we can attribute the sentiment to Dryden or simply to dramatic motivation, Troilus exclaims:

> Priesthood, that makes a merchandise of heaven!
> Priesthood, that sells even to their prayers and blessings,
> And forces us to pay for our own cozenage!

His prisoner Thersites agrees and carries the charge one step further:

> Nay, cheats heaven too with entrails and with offals;
> Gives it the garbage of a sacrifice,
> And keeps the rest for private luxury.

For these views Troilus sets him free: "Live; thou art honest, for thou hat'st a priest" (V.ii.).

21. Guilhamet, "Dryden's Debasement of Scripture in *Absalom and Achitophel*," *Studies in English Literature* 9 (1969): 395–413.

22. Dryden also makes here the familiar charges regarding clerical greed and political involvement; see esp. ll. 312–19 and 400–401: "*Levi*, thou art a load, I'll lay thee down, / And shew Rebellion bare, without a Gown." On the distribution of work on the poem see *Works*, 2:328.

23. Paulson, *The Fictions of Satire*, p. 120.

24. Ibid., p. 121.

25. See Dryden's *Vindication of The Duke of Guise*, in Scott-Saintsbury, 7:149. Of course, the facts of the historical narrative that he dramatized (Davila's) are such that Dryden had to depict the clergy's prominent role among the Guisards. But beyond the general necessity Dryden enjoyed much freedom in treating the clergy, and as a reading of his source shows he made the best of the opportunity. See also John Harrington Smith, "Some Sources of Dryden's Toryism, 1682–84," *Huntington Library Quarterly* 20 (1957): 233–43.

26. In the fourth scene, similarly, Dryden shows that the sermon is an effective instrument of sedition and rebellion. The later jibes at the clergy all occur early in Act Five, a section written by Dryden.

27. King, *Dryden's Major Plays* (New York: Barnes and Noble, 1966), p. 161.

28. Scott-Saintsbury, 6:410, 398. Cf. *The Laureat* (London, 1687): "Thy Pension lost" "strait a True Blue Protestant crept out; / The Fryar now was writ: and some will say / They smell a Male-Content through all the play" (p. 3).

29. King, *Dryden's Major Plays*, p. 161; Scott-Saintsbury, 6:397.

30. Cf. Dryden's remark in the Preface to *Religio Laici* that at least in comparison with the "Fanaticks" Papists are "the less dangerous (at least in appearance to our present State)." See also Dryden's treatment of Catholics in the Prologue to Southerne's *The Loyal Brother* (1682).

31. Louis I. Bredvold, "Political Aspects of Dryden's *Amboyna* and *The Spanish Fryar*," *Essays and Studies in English and Comparative Literature*, University of Michigan Publications, Language and Literature 8 (1932): 131.

32. In *Absalom and Achitophel* Dryden similarly extenuates Catholic

political intrigue. Is he trying to remove the smoke screen so that his audience can see clearly the real issues at stake in the current unrest? At any rate Dryden seems to go out of his way to establish that Dominic's superiors will suitably punish him; see IV.i. and V.ii. Clearly, Dryden's separation of the friar from politics is in the main an accurate depiction of the Restoration Catholic priesthood; see below, Chapter Five.

33. King, *Dryden's Major Plays*, p. 157.

34. Ibid., pp. 155–56.

35. Ward, *The Life of John Dryden*, p. 147.

36. Scott-Saintsbury includes the poem with the note that it was printed in the *State Poems* as "A Satire on Romish Confession by Mr. Dryden" (6:522–23). As is pointed out there, the poem is said in both the first edition and the folio of *The Spanish Fryar* to be "By a Friend of the Author's." Recent editors do not attribute the poem to Dryden.

37. In IV.i., for example, Dominic cries, "He has railed against the church, which is a fouler crime than the murder of a thousand kings."

38. David M. Vieth, "Concept as Metaphor: Dryden's Attempted Stylistic Revolution," *Language and Style* 3 (1970):198. See also Hoffman, *John Dryden's Imagery*, esp. pp. 73, 80.

39. *Works*, 17:225. Cf. Dryden's similar point in *The Hind and the Panther*:

> God's and kings rebels have the same good cause,
> To trample down divine and humane laws:
> Both wou'd be call'd Reformers, and their hate,
> Alike destructive both to church and state.
>
>   (1:357–60)

Dryden's clearest expressions of his political position, based in the belief that the king's authority derives from God, to whom alone he is responsible, are the well-known ll. 759–810 of *Absalom and Achitophel* and a passage in the Postscript to the translation of Maimbourg's *History of the League*; see *Works*, 18 (*The History of the League*, ed. Alan Roper [Berkeley: University of California Press, 1974]):393–94. We should observe, finally, that Dryden continues to believe in the superiority of the king's power over the church's power; he writes in the Dedication of *Plutarch's Lives*: "both our reformers of church and state pretend to a power superior to kingship. The fanatics derive their authority from the Bible, and plead religion to be antecedent to any secular obligation . . . they arrogate to themselves the right of disposing the temporal power according to their pleasure,—as that which is subordinate to the spiritual" (Scott-Saintsbury, 17:10).

40. Hoffman, *John Dryden's Imagery*, p. 80.

41. Cf. *The Duke of Guise:* "What, burn the tapers dim, / When glorious Guise, the Moses, Gideon, David, / The saviour of the nation, makes approach?" (I.i.) and "the new David, second Moses, / Prop of the church, deliverer of the people" (I.iii.). See Eric Voegelin, *The New Science of Politics* (Chicago: University of Chicago Press, 1952), p. 121. Note the frequent reference in the poem to "the publick Good" and its analogues. Voegelin's analysis of Puritan political psychology and the development of the "cause" is remarkably close to Dryden's treatment of Achitophel's methods in resuming the fight for "The Good old Cause" (l. 82); see pp. 135 ff. I have discussed these parallels in "The Ancients, the Moderns, and Gnosticism," *Studies on Voltaire and the Eighteenth Century* 151–55 (1976): esp. 161–66.

42. Dryden repeats the first phrase in the Dedication of *Plutarch's Lives*, where he charges that "the pretended Reformation of our Schismaticks, is to set up themselves in the Papal Chair" (*Works*, 17:231). Note the epigraph from *The Aeneid* which introduces the "Epistle to the Whigs," prefixed to the poem: "Per Graiûm *populos, mediaeque per Eldis Urbem* / *Ibat ovans;* Divum*que sibi poscebat Honores.*"

43. *Paradise Lost*, II.364–66. I quote from *The Poetical Works of John Milton*, ed. H. C. Beeching (Oxford: Clarendon Press, 1935).

44. To my knowledge only Ward has seriously considered this issue; though suggestive, his treatment is scanty. See *The Life of John Dryden*, esp. pp. 212–13.

45. *Works*, 17:231. Not surprisingly, Dryden argues in the Preface to *Religio Laici* that the Scriptures "are in themselves the greatest security of Governours, as commanding express obedience to them."

46. Cf. Dryden's claim in the Postscript to his translation of *The History of the League* that "the beginning of Leagues, Unions, and Associations, by those who call'd themselves Gods People, for Reformation of Religious Worship, and for the redress of pretended Grievances in the State, is . . . justly to be dated from *Luther's* time" (*Works*, 18:396).

47. Ibid.

48. *The Works of the Most Reverend Dr. John Tillotson* (London, 1696), p. 344. See also Edward Stillingfleet, *A Discourse Concerning the Nature and Grounds of the Certainty of Faith, in Answer to J. S. his Catholick Letters* (London, 1688), esp. p. 66. Cf. the frequent Protestant injunction "to search the Scriptures," as in Nicholas Stratford's *The Lay-Christian's Obligation to Read the Holy Scriptures* (London, 1687), p. 16.

49. Canes, *Fiat Lux* (London, 1661), p. 56. See Victor M. Hamm, "Dryden's *Religio Laici* and Roman Catholic Apologetics," *PMLA* 80 (1965):190–98. Comments like Canes's can be found in, for example,

Jacques-Bénigne Bossuet's *Exposition of the Catholic Church in Matters of Controversie* (London, 1686), p. 40.

50. *Works,* 18:399.

51. Ibid., p. 397. On this point, cf. Richard Hooker, *Works,* ed. Keble, 7th ed. (Oxford, 1888), esp. 1:145–55.

Chapter 4

1. Donald R. Benson has argued that Dryden was ignorant of the contents and direction of the *Critical History* ("Who 'Bred' *Religio Laici?,*" *Journal of English and Germanic Philology* 65 [1966]:238–51), and Phillip Harth has termed Dryden's explanation "fictitious" (*Contexts of Dryden's Thought,* p. 196). As to whether Dryden actually read Father Simon's "weighty" book, Swedenberg comments: "Dryden had ample time to examine the *Critical History* before writing *Religio Laici,* but it is unlikely that he gave his days and nights to a study of Father Simon before composing his poem" (*Works,* 2:343).

2. E. D. Hirsch, Jr., *Validity in Interpretation* (New Haven, Conn.: Yale University Press, 1967), p. 263.

3. Swedenberg briefly but helpfully notes some of the stylistic affinities between Horace's *Epistles* and *Religio Laici* (*Works,* 2:348–50). Harth recognizes that Dryden's poem assumes the form and structure of the Horatian epistle, which he describes as "loosely organized, informal poetic discourses scarcely suited to the development of closely reasoned logical proofs" (*Contexts of Dryden's Thought,* p. 56). But Harth contends that Dryden modifies the form and adapts it to the purpose of "logical arguments." The described modification is so extensive that little resemblance remains between the Latin poems and Dryden's, which is nevertheless still said to be a Horatian epistle.

4. Fraenkel, *Horace* (Oxford: Clarendon Press, 1957), p. 309.

5. *The Correspondence of Alexander Pope,* ed. George Sherburn (Oxford: Clarendon Press, 1959), 1:105; see also pp. 94, 346.

6. John Boswell, *A Method of Study: or, an Useful Library* (London, 1738), 1:273.

7. Brower, *Alexander Pope: The Poetry of Allusion* (Oxford: Clarendon Press, 1959), p. 175. Brower rightly observes that Horatian conversation, sometimes closer to lecture, proceeds not from doctrine but from "tone and dramatic exemplum" (p. 180). This holds true for *Religio Laici* as well. Satire I.x.9–14, which Pope used as epigraph for his *Epistles to Several Persons,* also summarizes the characteristics of Horace's *Epistles.*

8. The Dedication of the *Aeneis*, in *Essays of John Dryden*, ed. W. P. Ker (1900; rpt. Oxford: Clarendon Press, 1925), 2:215. Watson omits from his edition of the *Essays* the section in the Dedication containing this remark. Dryden quotes the line from Manilius which he had used as the epigraph for *Religio Laici*: "*Ornari res ipsa negat, contenta doceri.*"

9. A. W. Verrall speaks of the poem's "astounding commencement" (*Lectures on Dryden*, p. 155), and Walter Savage Landor is reported to have said, "Nothing was ever written in hymn equal to the beginning of Dryden's *Religio Laici*,—the first eleven lines" (*Diary, Reminiscences, and Correspondence of Henry Crabb Robinson*, ed. Thomas Sadler [Boston, 1870], 2:292).

10. Harth oddly contends that this section was originally a separate complimentary poem intended for inclusion in a new issue of the *Critical History* (*Contexts of Dryden's Thought*, pp. 174 ff.), but the mixed praise here, reflecting the speaker's wit, control, and proper intellectual and emotional distance and exactly suited to an epistle, would be inappropriate for an introductory poem, where the praise is expected to be undiluted.

11. Ibid., p. 197.

12. See Jean Steinmann, *Richard Simon et les origines de l'exégèse biblique* (Bruges: Desclée de Brouwer, 1960), and *The Diary and Correspondence of John Evelyn*, ed. John Forster (London, 1881), 3:264–65.

13. Cf. Swedenberg's description of the poem as "undogmatic, good-natured, urbane" (*Works*, 2:349).

14. Budick is less reductive than Harth though he appears to impose ideas on the poem; he thus argues for "the presence of certain ideas in the body of the poem that, when given their proper weight, may be seen to contribute to a poetic totality of great interest" (*Dryden and the Abyss of Light*, p. 73). My hope is to respect the poem's own movement and emphases, allowing it to establish the proper weight for the ideas treated.

15. Harth, *Contexts of Dryden's Thought*, p. 96. See also Donald J. Greene, " 'Logical Structure' in Eighteenth-Century Poetry," *Philological Quarterly* 31 (1962):315–36, and Jim W. Corder, "Rhetoric and Meaning in *Religio Laici*," *PMLA* 82 (1967):245–49.

16. Harth, *Contexts of Dryden's Thought*, p. 96.

17. See, esp., ibid., pp. 116–18, and Budick, *Dryden and the Abyss of Light*, pp. 93 ff. The simultaneous valuing and disvaluing of reason in the exordium and its relation to the whole has been ably discussed by Hoffman, *John Dryden's Imagery*, pp. 55–71. See also McHenry, "The Importance of Right Reason in Dryden's Conversion," which effectively

counters Budick's argument for innatist ideas in *Religio Laici,* and Jeanne K. Welcher, "The Opening of *Religio Laici* and Its Virgilian Associations," *Studies in English Literature* 8 (1968):391–96.

18. In addition to his contribution to *The Rehearsal,* Clifford wrote the vituperative *Notes upon Mr. Dryden's Poems in Four Letters,* dated 1672 and no doubt circulated in manuscript until publication in 1687, ten years after his death. I shall treat the controversy surrounding Clifford's *Treatise* at some length in the following chapter.

19. Harth, *Contexts of Dryden's Thought,* p. 235. Harth rejects E. N. Hooker's claim in "Dryden and the Atoms of Epicurus" (*ELH* 24 [1957]:177–90) that *Religio Laici* was a deliberate response to Clifford.

20. Clifford, *A Treatise of Humane Reason* (London, 1674), pp. 2–4. The quoted passage recalls Rochester's "Satyr against Mankind," esp. ll. 6–30; whether Clifford had his friend in mind in writing these lines is unknown, as is whether Rochester's imagery derives from Clifford. In any case, compare Budick's discussion of the exordium, which proposes Richard Burthogge's *Causa Dei* as an analogue (*Dryden and the Abyss of Light,* pp. 89 ff.).

21. Clifford, *Treatise,* pp. 4–6. Budick's argument, however, is that "*Religio Laici* turns inward" (p. 159).

22. With this point Dryden allows the Deist to notice a gap in the preceding argument (Dryden has appeared unduly scornful of the necessarily unsuccessful efforts of the Ancients). He will develop it in the Deist's "Objection" (ll. 168 ff.).

23. Arthur Friedman, "Pope and Deism (*The Dunciad,* iv. 459–92)," in *Pope and His Contemporaries: Essays Presented to George Sherburn,* ed. James L. Clifford and Louis A. Landa (Oxford: Clarendon Press, 1949), p. 92.

24. *The Case of Reason, or Natural Religion, Fairly and Fully Stated* (1713), in *The Works of the Reverend William Law* (Brockenhurst, 1891), 2:124.

25. That is to say, Dryden treats the Deist not simply for the sake of overcoming that position; except for brief mention at l. 115 the Deist does not reappear in ll. 99–167. Dryden's argument is clearly broader than a polemical defense of the Established Church. For a different view of the movement of the poetic argument, see Budick, who believes that the poem is "planned as a necessarily incomplete fulfillment of the blueprint in the exordium and as an exemplar of the formula that Dryden believed must be reversible. In both stages or situations that the poem can include it is man's reason, the taper of the Lord, that is developed into an assurance of man's ability to gain sufficient knowledge for salvation" (*Dryden and the Abyss of Light,* p. 97).

26. Harth, *Contexts of Dryden's Thought*, p. 141.

27. Dryden finds additional support for his appeal to God's mercy in Paul, paraphrasing Romans 2:14–15 in ll. 200–205. Largely on the basis of the last four verses of this paragraph,

> Then those who follow'd *Reasons* Dictates right;
> Liv'd up, and lifted high their *Natural Light;*
> With *Socrates* may see their Maker's Face,
> While Thousand *Rubrick-Martyrs* want a place.
>
> (ll. 208–11)

Budick has interpreted the poem as rationalistically exemplifying a belief, drawn from the Cambridge Platonists, in man's innate capacity for saving truths. If this were so, Dryden would not be so tentative here. Dryden is cautious and tentative because to be otherwise would convict him of the same assertiveness, dogmatism, and imposition of his own beliefs on God just condemned in the Deist. Dryden goes on to repeat his hope for non-Christians in the passage on Saint Athanasius, mentioned in the Preface (ll. 212–23); finding it "hard . . . to doom to *endless pains* / All who believ'd not" what the Bishop's zeal required (ll. 214–15), Dryden suggests that either we have traditionally misinterpreted Athanasius's meaning or else we should consider the harsh judgments rendered as a reflection of an emotional outburst, rather than as consistently held doctrine. One effect of Dryden's emphasis on charity in both poem and Preface is to suggest that a staunch believer in the power and prerogative of God can have at least some of the sensibilities flaunted by such men as the Deists.

28. See Vieth, "Concept as Metaphor: Dryden's Attempted Stylistic Revolution."

29. Harth and Budick disagree with each other about these lines. Harth believes that by ignorance Dryden refers to Catholicism, by pride to the sectarians, and Budick believes that the former suggests Deism, the latter term both Catholics and sectarians. As I have argued, it is not these few verses that are metaphorical but rather the entire series of arguments with the Deist, the Catholics, and the "Fanaticks."

30. Bredvold has mistaken for heartfelt yearning the irony and even sarcasm of ll. 282–83; see *The Intellectual Milieu of John Dryden.*

31. Up to this point Dryden had insinuated the problems that the *Critical History* had opened up for the author's own church, rather than confront the likelihood, noted by the priest himself, that the discovery of numerous important errors in the holy text seriously jeopardized the Protestant doctrine of *Scriptura sola.* By postponing this crucial consid-

eration Dryden effectively blunted the sensational and threatening point of Father Simon's argument; in addition, the treatment already given the priest and his work was designed to deny that the *Critical History* was destined to have monumental repercussions and so to undercut considerably the danger many thought it represented for Protestantism. See, though, "The Author's Preface Translated out of French," *A Critical History of the Old Testament,* trans. Henry Dickinson (London, 1682).

32. Cf. Sir Robert Howard, *The History of Religion* (London, 1694), esp. p. 120: "the imposing Humour of those who usurp more to themselves than belongs to Teachers, and the Quarrels and Disputes upon dark and unnecessary Notions, is an assuming what belongs to God. . . . By such Power assumed to themselves, they rob God of his Glory."

33. Lines 394–97 further link the pre- and post-Reformation situations; freed from the self-seeking tyranny of a vicious priesthood, the layman acts little less selfishly and irresponsibly.

34. Tillotson, *The Rule of Faith: or an Answer to the Treatise of Mr. I.S. entituled, Sure-footing, Etc.* (London, 1676), p. 106; Care, *Utrum Horum: or, The Nine and Thirty Articles of the Church of England, At large recited* . . . (London, 1682), p. 17.

35. *Two Letters of Advice, I. for the Susception of Holy Orders. II. for Studies Theological, especially such as are Rational* . . . (London, 1691), sigs. B3ʳ–B3ᵛ; the book was originally published in Dublin in 1672.

36. *The Several Ways of Resolving Faith By the Controvertists of the Roman and Reformed Religion,* 2d ed. (London, 1682), pp. 59–60.

37. On this and other points see the suggestive, and unduly neglected, essay by G. M. Turnell, "Dryden and the Religious Elements in the Classical Tradition," *Englische Studien* 70 (1935):244–61.

38. Evidently Dryden means "free of priestly control"—at least insofar as the Established Church disdained some of the authority vested in the priesthood by Rome. Because of the private nature of his stand, Dryden must once more indicate his willingness to submit "still" to his church. As in the Preface Dryden ties this submissiveness to a recognition of his own lack of ability; aware of his limitations, he shows a becoming deference to outside authority. The tension found elsewhere in the poem is not resolved here, however.

39. See Nicholas Stratford, *The Lay-Christian's Obligation to Read the Holy Scriptures* (London, 1687); Edward Stillingfleet, *A Discourse Concerning the Nature and Grounds of the Certainty of Faith, in Answer to J.S. his Catholick Letters* (London, 1688), esp. p. 66; and *The Works of the Most Reverend Dr. John Tillotson,* esp. the sermon "The Necessity of the

Knowledge of the Holy Scriptures." Unlike Dryden, Tillotson contends that if Scripture reading "be dangerous to any, none are so capable of doing mischief with it as the men of wit and learning" (p. 347).

40. As Earl Miner observes, "Tradition has of course some value, when genuine, but the tenor of Dryden's argument is such as to leave us feeling that the value is so compromised by dangers that one might best leave tradition, with due respect, on the shelf" (*Works*, 3 [*Poems 1685–1692*, ed. Earl Miner and Vinton A. Dearing (Berkeley: University of California Press, 1969)], 336). See also Budick, *Dryden and the Abyss of Light*, esp. pp. 81 and 157.

41. See, for example, Samuel Crossman's sermon *An Humble Plea for the Quiet Rest of God's Ark* (London, 1682), esp. p. 27, and George Hickes, *Two Treatises, One of the Christian Priesthood, The Other of the Dignity of the Episcopal Order* (London, 1707), esp. p. cxli: "the very same Artillery by which they have attempted to batter down the *Miter*, they will, if ever they see a Season for it, turn upon the Crown. The same way of reasoning will serve them as well against *Kingcraft*, and *Kings*, as *Priestcraft* and *Priests*."

42. See Empson's essays, "Dryden's Apparent Scepticism" and "A Deist Tract by Dryden."

43. It is worth noting that the anonymous *History of Whiggism, or, The Whiggish-Plots, Principles, and Practices, (Mining and Countermining the Tory-Plots and Principles)* . . . (London, 1682), suggests, somewhat like Dryden, that the clergy is at the bottom of the contention between Whigs and Tories, fanning the fires of disagreement. That in this and other ways Dryden shares the sentiments of those he opposes on other, larger grounds attests again to the precarious *via media* he has carved out.

Chapter 5

1. See, especially, Macaulay's view that Dryden "knew little and cared little about religion. . . . Finding that if he continued to call himself a Protestant his services would be overlooked, he declared himself a Papist" (*History of England* [London, 1849], 2:199) and W. D. Christie's comment that "it is hard to believe that in this great change . . . visions of greater worldly advantage did not influence Dryden" (*The Poetical Works of John Dryden* [London, 1870], p. lviii). The charge that the conversion brought Dryden worldly profit has proved completely unfounded; see, for example, Louis I. Bredvold, "Notes on John Dryden's Pension," *Modern Philology* 30 (1933):267–74.

2. See Miner's introduction to *The Hind and the Panther* in the third

volume of *Works,* as well as Miner's *Dryden's Poetry* (Bloomington: Indiana University Press, 1967), pp. 144–205, and Myers, "Politics in *The Hind and the Panther,*" *Essays in Criticism* 19 (1969):19–34.

3. Benson, "Theology and Politics in Dryden's Conversion," *Studies in English Literature* 4 (1964):403, 412.

4. McHenry, "The Importance of Right Reason in Dryden's Conversion," p. 84. See also Budick, *Dryden and the Abyss of Light,* esp. pp. 170–80.

5. Harth, *Contexts of Dryden's Thought,* p. 244.

6. Scott-Saintsbury, 1:261.

7. De Beer, "Dryden's Anti-Clericalism"; see above, Chapter Three.

8. *The Principles and Practices, Of certain Moderate Divines of the Church of England, (greatly mis-understood) Truly Represented and Defended* (London, 1670), pp. 8–9; though anonymous this tract is probably by Edward Fowler, a Latitudinarian.

9. Mistaken conclusions regarding the Latitudinarians have recently and effectively been challenged; see Margaret C. Jacob, *The Newtonians and the English Revolution, 1689–1720* (Ithaca, N.Y.: Cornell University Press, 1976), and Donald Greene, "Latitudinarianism and Sensibility: The Genealogy of the 'Man of Feeling' Reconsidered," *Modern Philology* 75 (1977):159–83.

10. *A Brief Account of the New Sect of Latitude-Men,* sig. A2^r, p. 14. The similarity between this statement and Dryden's in the Preface to *An Evening's Love* is apparent and important; see above, Chapter Two. See also *A Brief Account of the New Sect of Latitude-Men,* p. 20, and *Principles and Practices,* p. 296.

11. Glanvill, "Anti-fanatical Religion, and Free Philosophy. In a Continuation of the New Atlantis," in *Essays On Several Important Subjects In Philosophy and Religion* (London, 1676), pp. 12, 11. Before the revolution at least, the Latitudinarians were not inclined toward Whiggism; they were generally staunch defenders of Charles during the Exclusion Controversy, having been reduced politically to propagandists for the Crown; see Walter G. Simon, "The Restoration Episcopate and the Popish Plot," *Anglican Theological Review* 29 (1957):139–47, and *The Restoration Episcopate* (New York: Bookman, 1965).

12. Glanvill, *Essays,* p. 12.

13. *Principles and Practices,* p. 319.

14. Glanvill, *Essays,* p. 18.

15. Ibid., p. 26.

16. *Principles and Practices,* pp. 347, 316–17.

17. Glanvill, *Essays,* p. 25. The author of *Principles and Practices* approvingly says of the Latitudinarians, "I presume they would be very

glad, if our Church Doors were set wider open, I mean, if some things that most offend were taken out of the way; and that no such weight may be laid on any little things, as that they should be insisted on, to the endangering those of an higher nature, and hazarding the Churches prosperity and peace" (pp. 334–35).

18. Glanvill, *Essays*, p. 31.

19. George H. Tavard, *The Quest for Catholicity: A Study in Anglicanism* (New York: Herder and Herder, 1964), p. 123.

20. See Leonard J. Trinterud, "A.D. 1689: The End of the Clerical World," in *Theology in Sixteenth- and Seventeenth-Century England,* William Andrews Clark Memorial Library Seminar Papers (Los Angeles, 1971). The Latitudinarians thought that the liberal society they helped to create would need the church for its maintenance and support and that this would in turn insure a position for her—and themselves—as the dominant force in the religious life of the nation. Their means redounded on them, of course, for the alternative they offered to secularism and unbridled self-interest helped undermine the role they hoped to increase of the church in society.

21. Jacob, *The Newtonians and the English Revolution*, p. 22. See also Richard Schlatter, *The Social Ideas of Religious Leaders 1660–1688* (London: Oxford University Press, 1940). I am much indebted to both books.

22. Jacob, *The Newtonians and the English Revolution*, p. 70.

23. Ibid., p. 175.

24. It was the *vanity* of riches that disturbed the Broad Churchmen; see *The Diary of John Evelyn,* ed. E. S. de Beer (Oxford: Clarendon Press, 1955), 4:564, 584–86. On the Latitudinarians on public religion and self-interest, see, for example, John Tillotson, *Works to which is prefixed the Life of the Author by Thomas Birch* (London, 1752), 2:300–301, 3:53–55; John Wilkins, *Of the Principles and Duties of Natural Religion,* ed. Henry G. Van Leeuwen (New York: Johnson Reprint, 1969), pp. 168, 304–6, 312; *The Theological Works of Isaac Barrow,* ed. Alexander Napier (Cambridge, 1859), 1:177, 4:141, 7:158–59; Hezekiah Burton, *A Second Volume of Discourses* (London, 1685), p. 335.

25. Derham, *Physico-Theology: or, A Demonstration of the Being and Attributes of God, from His Works of Creation* (London, 1714), pp. 32–33. On distinctions between the physico-theologians and the Latitudinarians, see Phillip Harth, *Swift and Anglican Rationalism: The Religious Background of "A Tale of a Tub"* (Chicago: University of Chicago Press, 1961), pp. 23–24 n., 146 n.

26. *The Works of Richard Bentley,* ed. A. Dyce (London, 1838), 3:22, italics added.

27. Jacob, *The Newtonians and the English Revolution*, p. 181. With this

understanding of religion as public and social, argues Trinterud, perhaps too harshly, the Latitudinarians "turned away from the problems of sin, grace, sacraments, holy orders, and the like," directing their attention instead to "the social, political, and economic rewards of privilege and status. For other Latitudinarians what remained were the fields of literature, education, public service, philanthropy, and practical piety" ("A.D. 1689," p. 40).

28. Bentley, *Works*, 3:13.

29. Burnet, *An Exhortation to Peace and Union. A Sermon Preached at St. Lawrence-Jury, at the Election of the Lord-Mayor of London, On the 29th of September, 1681* (London, 1681), p. 3.

30. *The Works of the Most Reverend Dr. John Tillotson* (1696), p. 43.

31. *The Works Of the Most Reverend Dr. John Tillotson*, 2d ed. (London, 1717), pp. 89, 101, 102.

32. Burnet, *An Exhortation to Peace and Union*, pp. 21, 5, 10.

33. Scott-Saintsbury, 7:197; the discussion occurs in *The Vindication of The Duke of Guise*. Views similar to Hickes's are found in, among others, Henry Dodwell and Robert South.

34. Hickes, *Jovian, or, an Answer to Julian the Apostate* (London, 1683), p. 282.

35. Hickes, *A Letter Sent from beyond the Seas To One of the Chief Ministers of the Non-Conforming Party* . . . (n.p., 1674), p. 7.

36. Hickes, *The True Notion of Persecution Stated. In a Sermon Preach'd at the Time of the Late Contribution for the French Protestants*, 2d ed. (London, 1713), p. 168.

37. Hickes, *Some Discourses upon Dr. Burnet and Dr. Tillotson; Occasioned by the Late Funeral Sermon of the Former upon the Later* (London, 1695), p. 57.

38. Hickes, *Two Treatises*, p. 254.

39. Ibid., pp. ccxli, 131, 133.

40. *A Volume of Posthumous Discourses of the Late Reverend and Learned Dr. George Hickes* . . . (London, 1726), p. 386.

41. *The Constitution of the Catholick Church, and the Nature and Consequences of Schism, set forth In a Collection of Papers, written By the late R. Reverend George Hickes, D.D.* (London, 1716), pp. 138–39.

42. Ibid., p. 141.

43. Hickes, *Some Discourses upon Dr. Burnet and Dr. Tillotson*, sigs. A4^v-A4^r.

44. Ibid., p. 45.

45. Collins, *A Discourse of Free-Thinking* . . . (London, 1713), p. 172.

46. Paul C. Davies, "The Debate on Eternal Punishment in Late Sev-

enteenth- and Eighteenth-Century English Literature," *Eighteenth-Century Studies* 4 (1971):261.

47. *Several Letters Which passed between Dr. George Hickes, and a Popish Priest, Upon occasion of a Young Gentlewoman's Departing from the Church of England to that of Rome* (London, 1705), sig. C3ʳ, and *Christian Priesthood, and the Dignity of the Episcopal Order, Asserted and Defended*, 3d ed. (London, 1727), 1:xxi. Hickes claims a connection exists between anticlericalism and political radicalism, a connection Dryden showed to be unnecessary; see *Two Treatises*, p. cxli.

48. From a sermon perhaps misleadingly titled *The Ways of Pleasantness*, in *The Beauties of South, consisting of various and important extracts from the works of . . . R. South* (London, 1795), 1:23, italics added.

49. Jacob, *The Newtonians and the English Revolution*, p. 56.

50. Dryden's opposition to the clergy's involvement in politics in the works of this period may reflect, in part, opposition to the Latitudinarians' increasing role as political propagandists, even if on the side of the Court; see Simon, *The Restoration Episcopate*.

51. Harth, *Contexts of Dryden's Thought*, p. 235.

52. Ibid., p. 236.

53. Ibid., p. 238.

54. Ibid., p. 241.

55. "To Mr. Clifford. On His Humane Reason," in *The Dramatick Works Of his Grace George Villiers, Late Duke of Buckingham, With His Miscellaneous Poems, Essays and Letters* (London, 1715), 2:186–87. This spirited defense no doubt circulated in manuscript until its posthumous publication in 1705.

56. Warren, *An Apology for the Discourse of Humane Reason, Written by MA. Clifford, Esq; Being a Reply to Plain Dealing. With the Author's Epitaph and Character* (London, 1680), p. 126. See also pp. 127–28, 130.

57. Buckingham, *The Dramatick Works*, 2:187.

58. Harth, *Contexts of Dryden's Thought*, p. 242.

59. See *Reason Regulated: or, Brief Reflections, upon a late Treatise of Human-Reason* (n.p., 1675), pp. 22–25; A. M. (sometimes erroneously identified as Andrew Marvell), *Plain-Dealing: or, A full and particular Examination of a late Treatise, Entituled, Humane Reason* (London, 1675), pp. 34–35, 38; *The Spirit of Prophecie, wherein Is proved the Divine Authority of the Scripture, and Christian Religion . . .* (London, 1687), p. 220 (first published in 1679, with a slightly different title).

60. Warren, *An Apology*, p. 32, and Clifford, *Treatise*, p. 29.

61. Those exceptions are the Catholic author of *Reason Regulated*, who signed his pamphlet T. P., and the Cambridge Platonist George

Rust, whose *Discourse of the Use of Reason in Matters of Religion* (1683) his fellow "Anglican rationalist" Henry Hallywell prefaced. This book treats the Clifford position more sympathetically than any of the other Anglican attacks, and Hallywell defends Rust against the same notion that he has emphasized private reason at the expense of church authority. Like Harth but unlike Swedenberg in his commentary on *Religio Laici* in the second volume of the *Works*, I do not include in the controversy *The Interest of Reason in Religion* (1675) by the Dissenter and political radical Robert Ferguson.

62. The first was *The Natural Fanatick* (1676). See also *Reason Regulated*, pp. 22–25, 33, and, for other resemblances of Latitudinarianism, Warren, *An Apology*, pp. 38–39.

63. *Plain-Dealing*, p. 159. See Harth, *Contexts of Dryden's Thought*, and Hooker, "Dryden and the Atoms of Epicurus," pp. 177–90. Harth is mistaken in thinking that "every one of [Clifford's] opponents concentrates on the religious issues he has raised, either ignoring or briefly dismissing the political corollary of his position" (p. 237).

64. Warren, *An Apology*, p. 114.

65. Clifford, *Treatise*, pp. 84–85, 15–16; see also pp. 66–67.

66. *Plain-Dealing*, pp. 98–99, 10, 50–51; see also *Reason Regulated*, p. 72.

67. *Reason Regulated*, p. 38.

68. Warly, *The Natural Fanatick, or, Reason Considered in Its Extravagancy in Religion, and (in some late Treatises) Usurping the Authority of the Church and Councils* (London, 1676), sig. A3ᵛ.

69. *The Spirit of Prophecie*, p. 218.

70. *Reason Regulated*, pp. 27, 45.

71. Ibid., pp. 19–20.

72. Miller, *Popery and Politics in England, 1660–1688* (Cambridge: Cambridge University Press, 1973), p. 48.

73. Ibid., p. 30.

74. *Reflexions upon the Oathes of Supremacy and Allegiance* (London, 1661), pp. 61–62; quoted in Miller, *Popery and Politics*, p. 31.

75. *Sir John Winter's Observations upon the Oath enacted 1 Eliz. commonly called, the Oath of Supremacy . . .* (London, 1679), pp. 17–18; quoted in Miller, *Popery and Politics*, pp. 31–32.

76. *Cavalier: Letters of William Blundell to his Friends, 1620–1698*, ed. Margaret Blundell (London: Longmans, 1933), pp. 202–3.

77. Cressy, *Exomologesis: or, A Faithfull Narration of The Occasion and Motives of the Conversion unto Catholike Unity . . .* (Paris, 1653), pp. 471–72. This book was first published in 1647.

78. Turnell, "Dryden and the Religious Elements," p. 246.

79. *Works,* 17:225; Miller, *Popery and Politics,* p. 110.

80. *Rushworth's Dialogues. Or, The Judgment of common sence in the Choyce of Religion. Last Edition, Corrected and enlarg'd by Thomas White, Gent.* (Paris, 1654), pp. 226, 227. Whether this work is mainly White's or William Rushworth's is unclear.

81. Quoted in Miller, *Popery and Politics,* p. 172.

82. George Savile, 1st Marquis of Halifax, *Complete Works,* ed. J. P. Kenyon (Harmondsworth: Penguin, 1969), p. 106.

83. *Works,* 3:340.

84. *The Question of Questions, which Rightly Resolv'd resolves All our Questions in Religion. The Question is, Who ought to be our Judge in all these Differences?,* 2d ed. (London, 1687), p. 221; this book was originally published in 1658. For Clifford's claim that God "commands no more but to search, and ye shall find," see *Treatise,* pp. 66–70.

85. *Reason Regulated,* p. 33.

86. Bossuet, *An Exposition of the Catholic Church in Matters of Controversie,* p. 40.

87. Miller, *Popery and Politics,* p. 18.

88. Sergeant, *Sure-Footing in Christianity, or Rational Discourses on The Rule of Faith,* 2d ed. (London, 1665), p. 87.

89. Cressy, *Exomologesis,* p. 411.

90. *Rushworth's Dialogues,* pp. 149, 59.

91. See Hooker, "Dryden and the Atoms of Epicurus," and Hamm, "Dryden's *Religio Laici* and Roman Catholic Apologetics."

92. Cressy, *Exomologesis,* pp. 61, 23, 162, 168, 466, 276, 277.

93. *Works,* 3:336–37. On this point Miner differs from Harth, who believes that Dryden was unsympathetic as a Catholic to the "radical" party in his new church, the so-called Blackloists, "whose 'new Rule of Faith' consist[ed] entirely of tradition, to the exclusion of Scripture" (*Contexts of Dryden's Thought,* p. 254). See also Harth's "Religion and Politics in Dryden's Poetry and Plays," *Modern Philology* 70 (1973):236–42. In the present chapter I have cited passages from both sides in the Catholic controversy.

94. Miller, *Popery and Politics,* p. 208.

Chapter 6

1. See Ward, *The Life of John Dryden,* pp. 219–20.

2. *The Letters of John Dryden,* ed. Charles E. Ward (Durham, N.C.: Duke University Press, 1942), p. 123; hereafter cited as *Letters.*

3. I thus disagree with Phillip Harth, who writes: "The fact is that

the Anglican and Catholic positions on the issues debated in the second parts of *Religio Laici* and *The Hind and the Panther* are totally inconsistent" (*Contexts of Dryden's Thought*, p. 227). See Budick, *Dryden and the Abyss of Light*, p. 172.

4. Other parallels include 1:122 ff., with the Preface, and 2:185, with the central concern of *Religio Laici*.

5. *Works*, 3:336–37. On these points see also Harth's *Contexts of Dryden's Thought*; Miner's correction in *Works*, 3:337 n.; and Harth's reply in "Religion and Politics in Dryden's Poetry and Plays."

6. *Works*, 3:337.

7. Cf. *The Medall*, ll. 279–80, where Dryden refers to Shaftesbury's perhaps Deistic, perhaps Epicurean, God as "A jolly God, that passes hours too well / To promise Heav'n, or threaten us with Hell."

8. Cf. Dryden's contrasting description of Catholicism in *A Defence of the Papers:* "Ask even our Protestant Gentlemen at their return from Catholic Countries, and they cannot but confess, that the Exercises of their Devotion, their Mortifications, their Austerities, their Humility, their Charity, and in short, all the ways of good living are practis'd there in a far greater measure than they are in *England:* but these are the Vertues from which we are blessedly reform'd by the Example and Precept of that Lean, Mortified Apostle, St. *Martin Luther"* (*Works*, 17:301).

9. See also the Hind's moving passage at 3:281–84, from which Dryden himself seems little distanced as he bids "a long farwell to worldly fame."

10. In *A Defence of the Papers* Dryden asserted that "a Latitudinarian . . . in plain terms, is no otherwise different from a Presbyterian, than by *whatsoever Titles and Dignities he is distinguish'd"* (*Works*, 17:304). See also ibid., p. 292.

11. The reference is to John "Century" White's *The First Century of Scandalous Malignant Priests;* see *Works*, 3:431.

12. As a result of events ushered in by the "glorious" triumph of the House of Orange, according to Trinterud, God virtually became "a free option" ("A.D. 1689," p. 39). See also George Every, *The High Church Party 1688–1718* (London: SPCK, 1956), p. xiii. The "Glorious Revolution" was for Dryden the implementation of those principles he had long reprobated. For Dryden's later political views, see, for example, "To My Honour'd Kinsman, John Driden."

13. *Essays*, 2:284.

14. Probably the strongest outburst in these works occurs in *Cleomenes,* but it is uttered by the Hobbesian Cassandra and so, especially since it receives no support from other characters, may be viewed as at

least partly dramatic. In any case, the passage seems aimed at the materialism of the Anglican clergy reprobated elsewhere:

> Fat offerings are the priesthood's only care;
> They take the money, and heaven hears the prayer.
> Without a bribe their oracles are mute;
> And their instructed gods refuse the suit.
>
> (III.ii.)

15. Scott-Saintsbury, 7:296; but see also John Robert Moore, "Political Allusions in Dryden's Later Plays," *PMLA* 73 (1958):36–42.

16. Dryden may be attempting to correct the imbalance apparent in his treatment of clergymen over the years; later on in the essay he acknowledges Luke Milbourne's criticism of his abuse of the clergy and proceeds to ask pardon of "good priests." The sentences that follow in the long passage quoted in the text, insisting on the need for an external, impartial critic of the clergy, seem largely a response to the counterattack on priest-baiting by Collier.

17. *Essays*, 2:282–84.

18. *Works*, 3:445.

19. See Charles Dahlberg, "Chaucer's Cock and Fox," *Journal of English and Germanic Philology* 53 (1954):277–90.

20. Citations of "The Cock and the Fox" and "The Character of a Good Parson" are to Kinsley, *Poems*. All citations to this edition are given in the text by line numbers and preceded by "K."

21. Miner, *Dryden's Poetry*, p. 313.

22. On the linking of the Fox and Puritanism, see Scott-Saintsbury, 11:355, and Kinsley, *Poems*, 4:2076. Lines 480–502 introduce the Fox in terms that echo the portrait of Shimei in *Absalom and Achitophel*, which suggests that Dryden wishes us to note the self-interested and essentially hypocritical nature of the Puritanism that threatens to consume the Anglican clergy and with it the Established Church as a possible *via media*.

23. *Letters*, pp. 115–16.

24. Ibid., p. 44; see also p. 160 n.

25. Though I am not prepared to argue for it as an occasion of Dryden's poem, I think the "Good Parson" is illuminated by juxtapositon with Edmund Hickeringill's *The Lay-Clergy: or, The Lay-Elder. In a Short Essay in Answer To this Query; Whether it be Lawful for Persons in Holy Orders to Exercise Temporal Offices, Honours, Jurisdictions and Authorities . . .* (London, 1695), which answers in the affirmative, unlike Dryden, and

which deemphasizes differences between clergy and laity and so diminishes what Dryden hopes to secure: the important role of the clergy as exemplars of the Christian religion.

26. These last two couplets suggest a parallel with Dryden's own situation.

27. Others at the time cited Chaucer's Parson as an exemplary priest. In his discussion of the conditions of the Restoration priesthood, the author of *A Modest Plea for the Clergy* (London, 1677), apparently Lancelot Addison, quotes the portrait and concludes, not unlike Dryden, that there is "nothing doth more effectually imprint the *Lessons* of Holiness and Vertue upon the people, than the exemplary Conversation of their Teacher" (p. 160). For a discussion of contemporary views of Chaucer and the Wycliffe era, see Austin C. Dobbins, "Dryden's 'Character of a Good Parson': Background and Interpretation," *Studies in Philology* 53 (1956): 51–59.

28. Citations from Chaucer are to *The Works of Geoffrey Chaucer*, ed. F. N. Robinson, 2d ed. (Boston: Houghton Mifflin, 1961). I quote ll. 481–84 of the General Prologue.

29. James Kinsley has argued, however, that Bishop Thomas Ken was Dryden's model ("Dryden's *Character of a Good Parson* and Bishop Ken," *Review of English Studies*, n.s., 3 [1952]: 155–58).

30. Whereas it is true that in the Preface to *Tyrannick Love* Dryden seems to distinguish between the priestly order and the men who comprise it, he appears at that point to be mainly rationalizing; a defensive tone appears throughout the passage. Surely we are justified in maintaining that even if Dryden did make this distinction all along (which is unlikely), he never felt its significance so deeply or understood it so fully as later in his career.

Index